Six Ways to Destroy Your Life

And the Life-Saving Alternatives

Jonathan Macintyre

DEDICATION

Being the first work that I have published, I dedicate this book to my beloved wife, Courtney, who is my closest companion and my very best of friends, and who has ceaselessly encouraged me and stuck with me throughout this adventure, and has given me countless great ideas along the way.

CONTENTS

ACKNOWLEDGMENTS

I want to thank my wife, Courtney, for editing the book for me, and for encouraging me to take up this task for the Lord and His people. Thanks to my beloved brothers in Christ, Joe Martinez and David Judd, for graciously editing the book for me and giving me excellent feedback. I want to thank my parents for "training me up in the way I should go," which had a strong influence on the writing of this book. I am forever grateful to you both. Thank you to my seminary professors for all the time they poured into me for several years, equipping and encouraging me to become a better writer. A big thank you to Tom Fay for his wonderful support and the role he played in encouraging me to write this book. Last but most importantly, I want to thank the Lord for His grace and goodness to me and for giving me the inspiration for this book and directing me along the way. All glory to Him alone.

Introduction

Maybe you were surprised, suspicious, humored, or intrigued when reading the title of this book. Maybe you're asking, "Why write a book with such a negative, depressing title? This won't sell. The author really doesn't know how to market himself." Good question. After all, we often hear of books with much more positive titles such as "Eight Ways to Live Healthier," "Five Ways to be Successful in Life," "Ten Ways to Live Happily Ever After," and so on.[1] Not that there is anything inherently wrong with such titles (depending on the content of the book), but I simply wanted to go outside the norm and capture people's attention with not only a strikingly different kind of title, but a different kind of content as well. So, if your attention was caught or your interest piqued when reading the title of this book, I have succeeded. If I didn't capture your attention, well, read the book anyway.

It's important when discussing any topic to make sure that we have a proper understanding of the terms being used. It's crucial for an author to define his terms in order to avoid being misunderstood and to help people not to misinterpret or misapply what he's saying to them. Thus, right off the bat we need to have a good working definition of the word *destroy* before we go any further, as this is a major theme of the book. The word *destroy* has several meanings. The primary way that I will use this word throughout this book is *to ruin emotionally, spiritually, physically, mentally, etc.*

---

[1] To my knowledge, these are all made up titles, not titles of actual books.

The purpose of this book is to use many of the proverbs of King Solomon to warn readers of the consequences of living foolishly and to exhort you to live wisely. Though we can't change people's hearts, we can at least warn them of the effects of their decisions and lifestyles. Therefore, this book serves as an instruction manual, warning readers of the destructive consequences of living foolishly and then teaching them the healthy, life-saving alternatives to living foolishly. How will we accomplish this?

There are 12 chapters in this book. The odd number chapters focus on specific sins that Solomon says will destroy your life. Each of these chapters will begin with a verse(s) from Proverbs that serves as the theme verse for the chapter. And you will do well to note that every theme verse shares one common theme: destruction. The person who practices any of these sins will be destroyed. Hence, the title of this book being *6 Ways to Destroy Your Life*. Many of these theme verses compare and contrast the wise person and the fool. In one half of the verse, Solomon mentions the theme sin and the consequences that come with that sin. Then, in the other half of the verse, Solomon provides us with what I call the life-saving alternative. The structure of this book will follow Solomon's pattern: the odd number chapters will focus on the destructive sins, while the even number chapters will examine the life-saving alternative to those sins.

One final note: the main audience for this book is Christians of all ages who are seeking to walk in the ways of the Lord and want to avoid destroying their lives through sinful living.

May you be blessed as you read this book, may you grow in the grace and knowledge of Jesus Christ, may you be challenged, and may you be changed soli deo Gloria.

1

REJECT WISDOM, EMBRACE DESTRUCTION

Because I have called and you refused,
I have stretched out my hand and no one regarded,
Because you disdained all my counsel,
And would have none of my rebuke,
I also will laugh at your calamity;
I will mock when your terror comes,
When your terror comes like a storm,
And your destruction comes like a whirlwind,
When distress and anguish come upon you.

Proverbs 1:24-27

But he who sins against me wrongs his own soul;
All those who hate me love death.

Proverbs 8:36

This first chapter really sets the stage for the rest of the book. So many of the sins that are covered in the following chapters come as a result of a lack of godly wisdom. For example, we'll see that there is a direct relation between rejecting wisdom and being unteachable (chapter 9). There's also a direct correlation between a lack of wis-

dom and having a prideful attitude (chapter 10). Having bad friendships (chapter 8) goes hand-in-hand with a lack of wisdom. And
the list goes on.

If you're looking for ways to destroy your life, the wise King Solomon has prescribed a simple solution for you: simply hate and reject wisdom.

What's So Great About Wisdom?

This question is one that shouldn't be treated flippantly. In his *Soliloquies*, Saint Augustine references Cornelius Celsus and says that
"wisdom is the greatest good."[2] Why all the hype about wisdom,
and why is it so important that we be filled with it? Let's partially
answer these questions by taking a look at what the wisest man
who ever lived (except Jesus) thought about wisdom.

When Solomon was still a young man, his father King David died,
and thus Solomon became king of Israel, which was a very great
and powerful nation at the time. There was a lot of pressure on
Solomon to live up to his father's greatness and to be a good king.
But he was young, inexperienced, and he didn't have a clue what he
was doing. One night, God appeared to Solomon in a dream and
said, "Ask! What shall I give you?" (2 Chron 1:7) Imagine that!
God appears to *you* and basically tells you to ask for anything you
want. It's like God is writing a blank check for you. What would be
your request? All the money in the world? Fame? Power? To be the
most attractive person ever? To own the planet? What did Solomon request? Verses 8-10 tell us:

> And Solomon said to God: "You have shown great mercy
> to David my father, and have made me king in his place.
> Now, O LORD God, let Your promise to David my father

---

[2] Saint Augustine, *The Soliloquies of St. Augustine* trans. by Rose
Elizabeth Cleveland (Boston, MA: Little, Brown, and Company, 1910),
37.

be established, for You have made me king over a people like the dust of the earth in multitude. Now give me wisdom and knowledge, that I may go out and come in before this people; for who can judge this great people of Yours?"

Out of every possible thing he could've requested, Solomon asked for *wisdom*. Why did he choose wisdom above all else? What does Solomon's request tell us about his view of wisdom? Obviously, he saw it as being invaluable, of great necessity and enormous worth something to be treasured above all else. Where and from whom did he get such an esteemed view of wisdom? It was from his father, David.

In Proverbs 4:3-9, Solomon not only recounts for us what David told him about wisdom when he was still very young, but he also answers our question about what is so great about having wisdom:

> When I was my father's son, tender and the only one in the sight of my mother, he also taught me, and said to me: "Let your heart retain my words; keep my commands, and live. Get wisdom! Get understanding! Do not forget, nor turn away from the words of my mouth. Do not forsake her, and she will preserve you; love her, and she will keep you. Wisdom *is* the principal thing; *therefore* get wisdom. And in all your getting, get understanding. Exalt her, and she will promote you; she will bring you honor, when you embrace her. She will place on your head an ornament of grace; a crown of glory she will deliver to you."

What's so great and important about wisdom? According to these verses it will preserve and protect you, it will guard you from harm and foolishness, and it will bring you promotion and honor in life as well as glory and grace. But the principal—or main, most important—thing is that you must *get* wisdom. It isn't enough to *know* that wisdom is important; you must *get it* yourself and hold onto it. Notice the various commands David issues to Solomon concerning wisdom: *do not forsake her, love her, exalt her, embrace her, do not forget.* In essence, David is saying the same thing in many different ways; namely, he's commanding his son to cherish, seek, and cling to wisdom. And no wonder David says to do this, considering all the effects it'll have on one's life.

So, Solomon's one request of God was for wisdom. What was God's response? Second Chronicles 1:11-12 tell us:

> Then God said to Solomon: "Because this was in your heart, and you have not asked riches or wealth or honor or the life of your enemies, nor have you asked long life—but have asked wisdom and knowledge for yourself, that you may judge My people over whom I have made you king— wisdom and knowledge *are* granted to you; and I will give you riches and wealth and honor, such as none of the kings have had who *were* before you, nor shall any after you have the like."

You can't beat that deal! God was well-pleased with Solomon's request for wisdom. Solomon's priorities were right on target.

As you continue through this chapter, you'll find many other ways in which wisdom is so great which should lead you into an understanding of why it's so important for you to possess it.

A lack and/or hatred of wisdom will lead to your destruction, as is clearly stated in the verses at the opening of this chapter. In these verses, wisdom is personified as a woman speaking to a foolish young man. She says that the foolish young man hated her and, as a result, he would be destroyed. In order to understand why a lack and/or hatred of wisdom will lead to your destruction, it's important to begin by having a good grasp on what wisdom is in the first place.

What is Wisdom?

Wisdom can simply be defined as the proper application of knowledge. It isn't enough to *know* truth; truth must be applied correctly, and this is wisdom. For example, you might have knowledge that it's a really bad idea to play football in the middle of the freeway while cars are screaming by at high speeds. That knowledge is essential, but it isn't enough. Wisdom properly *applies* that knowledge and says, "I'm not going to play football in the freeway." Wisdom means to have good judgment and to make good choices in light of the knowledge you possess.

It should be noted that in the context of the Book of Proverbs, wisdom is something to be sought after and gained, often implying that one doesn't currently possess it. Since we don't naturally possess it, we must seek to obtain it. This is why Solomon says on multiple occasions, "Get wisdom" (Prov 2:4, 10; 4:5, 7). It's important to understand this in order to get a good grasp on what it means to hate wisdom.

Hating Wisdom

In the context of Proverbs, to hate wisdom implies that you don't currently *have* wisdom and that you're neglecting either to receive it from someone or to pursue it yourself. Another way of saying it is that Dylan (our made-up character for the moment) doesn't have wisdom, but he needs it. He's either being offered wisdom from someone else or he is being encouraged to seek for it himself. The point is that Dylan doesn't currently have wisdom, but there is something (or someone) telling him that he needs it. Therefore, he needs to *do something* in order to get wisdom, whether it be listening to someone and being teachable and receiving the wisdom they're providing, or devoting himself to the pursuit of attaining wisdom. To *hate* wisdom, then, is to either *reject* or *neglect* it.

To *reject* something implies that something is being offered to you.

Therefore, to reject wisdom implies that someone is offering wisdom to you and you're choosing to refuse it. In the case of Proverbs 1:20-25 and 29-30, the young man to whom (personified) wisdom is speaking is rejecting her offer (note such words and phrases as *refused, disdained, would have none of my reproof, hated,* and *despised*).

On the other hand, to *neglect* something usually tends to mean that you are *putting off* doing something you should do. In other words, you aren't giving the proper attention that is due to a necessary task. In the case of Proverbs 1:24 and 28, it appears that the young man neglected—or put off—a personal pursuit of attaining wisdom (note the phrase *no one regarded*).

What does it look like, practically speaking, to hate wisdom? Answering this question is not all that difficult. Here's a simple three-step method for figuring out what hating wisdom looks likes on a practical level: (1) examine how a wise person lives, (2) examine what (in the Book of Proverbs) wisdom offers to people and what she commands them to do, and then (3) simply consider what are the complete opposites of (1) and (2), i.e., examine the opposite habits of a wise person's lifestyle, and examine the opposite—or negative—ways to respond to what wisdom offers.

Take Proverbs 14:16, for example. Solomon says, "A wise man is cautious and turns away from evil." Let's apply (1) and (3) of the three-step method: (1) how does a wise person live? He is careful and shuns evil; (3) what is the opposite of this? To live recklessly and to run toward evil and indulge in it.

As another example, consider Proverbs 8:6-7 in which Solomon is again personifying wisdom. She (wisdom) says, "Listen, for I will speak of excellent things, and from the opening of my lips *will come* right things; for my mouth will speak truth." Let's apply (2) and (3) of the three-step method: (2) what is it that wisdom is demanding of and offering to people? She's commanding them to listen to her, and she's offering excellent and right things and truth to those who heed her; (3) what is the opposite of these things? To reject wisdom is to welcome lies as well as bad, evil things into one's life. These are two illustrations of how the three-step method works. I encourage you to employ it while reading through Proverbs.

Let's apply this three-step method as we examine what Solomon says in Proverbs concerning wisdom. See the table on pages 8-11 that compares the wise versus the foolish person. This will help you to better see what it looks like to hate wisdom.

The Wise Man and the Fool

The opposite of wisdom is foolishness. Most of Solomon's proverbs consist of comparing and contrasting wisdom and foolishness. Therefore, to answer the question of what it looks like to hate wisdom, let's start by examining some of the proverbs that directly compare the wise man to the fool. Studying how the foolish man—the polar opposite of wise man—lives is the key to finding out what it looks like to hate wisdom. I have included a helpful chart on pages 8-11 that looks at sample proverbs and identifies how each one describes the wise and the fool. I recommend carefully studying the chart and then examining your heart to see whether any of the characteristics of the foolish person are descriptive of you.[3]

Practical Ways to Show a Hatred of Wisdom

Here are just three of the many ways in which you can expressly show a hatred of wisdom: be unteachable, make foolish friendships, and be prideful.

---

[3] This is not an all-inclusive list. Often in Proverbs, Solomon compares the wise and the fool by using the terms *the righteous* and *the wicked*. For your own personal study, read through Proverbs and make a list of the comparisons between the righteous and the wicked. Doing this will give you a much more detailed idea of how the wise person lives versus how the foolish person lives, as well as the consequences of each lifestyle.

Proverb:	Wise:	Fool:	How to Hate Wisdom:
9:8 "Do not correct a scoffer, lest he hate you; rebuke a wise *man,* and he will love you."	Appreciates correction	Hates the person who rebukes him/her	Be unteachable; hate rebuke and correction; surround yourself with yes men.
10:14 "Wise *people* store up knowledge, but the mouth of the foolish *is* near destruction." (See also 15:14)	Treasures, seeks to attain, and stores up knowledge.	Speaks foolishness	Say foolish things, speak before you think, slander others. Basically, mimic the way a fool speaks.
10:19 "In the multitude of words sin is not lacking, but he who restrains his lips *is* wise."	Chooses words carefully, thinks before he/she speaks, practices self-restraint when speaking.	Is careless with his/her words.	Have no filter on your mouth, talk a lot, speak without thinking.
10:23 NLT "Doing wrong is fun for a fool, but living wisely brings pleasure to the sensible."	Finds pleasure and joy in living wisely.	Finds pleasure in doing evil. Doing wicked things is considered sport. It's all a joke. (Prov. 14:9)	View sin with the total opposite perspective than God's perspective. Treat sin like a joke.

12:15 "The way of a fool *is* right in his own eyes, but he who heeds counsel *is* wise." (See also 17:10)	Is teachable, appreciates and heeds wise counsel.	Is unteachable, stuck in his/her ways, arrogantly thinks his/her wrong opinion is right. Is delusional.	Be unteachable, reject good, wise counsel, and always think your way is the right way.
12:16 NLT "A fool is quick-tempered, but a wise person stays calm when insulted." (See also 14:29)	Keeps his/her cool when annoyed or insulted, "overlooks and insult" (NET), exercises fruit of the Spirit (e.g., self-control), and practices love: "Love is not easily angered or resentful" (1 Cor 13:5 NET).	Has a very short temper, is easily and quickly angered by others, takes offense easily, and his/her "annoyance is known at once" (NET).	Don't practice self-control, have no rule over your own spirit (Prov 25:28), be thin-skinned, get offended easily, act impulsively, and think of yourself more highly than you ought.
12:23 NLT "The wise don't make a show of their knowledge, but fools broadcast their foolishness." (See also 15:2, 7)	Isn't boastful/showy about what he/she knows.	Boisterously blurts out and broadcasts to everyone that he/she is a fool.	Don't be humble, but be loud and obnoxious and make sure everyone hears you all the time.
13:1 "A wise son *heeds* his father's instruction, but a scoffer does not listen to rebuke." (See also 15:20)	Listens to parents and is teachable and respectful.	Is unteachable and disrespectful to parents.	Practice a lifestyle of disobedience to the fifth commandment, i.e., dishonor your parents.

13:16 "Every prudent *man* acts with knowledge, but a fool lays open *his* folly."	Is well-informed and avoids acting in/with ignorance. They "think before they act" (NLT). Actions are based in knowledge, not on feelings/whims.	Lays out his/her foolishness for all to see, and even "brags about" (NLT) and "flaunts" (ESV) his/her foolishness.	Remember: wisdom is the proper application of knowledge. Wisdom is rooted in knowledge. If you don't have knowledge, you can't act wisely. Therefore, in order to hate wisdom, make your decisions based on anything (e.g., feelings, emotions, desires) but knowledge.
14:8 NIV "The wisdom of the prudent is to give thought to their ways, but the folly of fools is deception."	Ponders and thinks seriously about his/her actions and lifestyle in order to correct wrong habits and live wiser.	Deceives him/herself into thinking that his/her own way is right.	Don't give serious thought to your thoughts, words, and actions. Live absent-mindedly of your actions and their consequences.
14:16 NASB "A wise man is cautious and turns away from evil, but a fool is arrogant and careless."	Is careful about his/her ways, gives serious thought to his/her actions and lifestyle, and shuns evil	Is arrogant, "self-confident" (NKJV), "reckless (ESV), "hotheaded" (NIV), and "throws off restraint and is overconfident" (NET)	Avoid caution and be careless/reckless. Be arrogant, think of yourself more highly than you ought, and indulge in sin.

18:2 "A fool has no delight in understanding, but in expressing his own heart." (See also 28:26 and 29:11)	Implication for the wise: he/she practices self-restraint and is careful not to verbalize everything on the mind and in the heart.	Is careless about and lacks all desires for obtaining wisdom and understanding, and chooses rather to spout everything that is in his/her heart.	Verbalize everything on your heart and mind. Don't have a filter. Some wise advice: keep in mind Jeremiah 17:9 and act accordingly, "The heart is deceitful above all things and desperately wicked."
21:20 *"There is desirable treasure, and oil in the dwelling of the wise, but a foolish man squanders it."*	Saves his/her money, is frugal, and is wise with money and possessions.	Is like the prodigal son, squandering, and quickly using up whatever he/she has.	Don't save your money, have unhealthy spending habits, and blow it all on worthless stuff.
26:11 "As a dog returns to his own vomit, so a fool repeats his folly."	Implication for the wise: learns from his/her mistakes and doesn't repeat them.	Doesn't learn from his/her past mistakes and, therefore, is doomed to repeat them.	Don't give thought to your ways, disregard the fact that failure is often the best teacher.

Be Unteachable

A careful examination of Proverbs 1:20-27 reveals that hating wisdom is closely connected to despising instruction and correction, i.e., being unteachable. In verses 22 and 23, personified wisdom declares, "How long, you simple ones, will you love simplicity? For scorners delight in their scorning, and fools hate knowledge. Turn at my rebuke; surely I will pour out my spirit on you; I will make my words known to you." Wisdom is here attempting to reprove and instruct the naïve, simple-minded person in the right way, the way of wisdom. In essence, she is saying, "Stop being foolish and naïve. Listen to me, and you'll be blessed."

Clearly, given the context of this passage, the naïve person didn't heed the words of wisdom: "Because I have called and *you refused* [emphasis added], I have stretched out my hand and *no one regarded* [emphasis added], because *you disdained all my counsel* [emphasis added], and *would have none of my rebuke* [emphasis added]" (Prov 1:24-25). According to this passage, there's a direct connection between hating wisdom and despising necessary rebuke and instruction. So then, if you want to destroy your life, it's simple: just hate wisdom and hate the rebuke and instruction that she gives.

Foolish Friendships

Another way in which people can express a hatred of wisdom is by the company they keep. In Proverbs 13:20 Solomon says, "He who walks with wise *men* will be wise, but the companion of fools will be destroyed." As I will discuss in further detail in chapter seven, you become like the company you keep. Generally, people who intentionally surround themselves with wise people do so for a reason: to become wiser. In contrast, he who chooses to be a "companion of fools" is sending a pretty obvious message: he either doesn't *care about* wisdom or he doesn't *want* wisdom, and the consequences are devastating.

Solomon's son, Rehoboam, is a perfect example of rejecting wise counselors and being a companion of fools. After Solomon died, Rehoboam succeeded him to the throne. In 1 Kings 12:3-14, the nation Israel came before King Rehoboam and made a reasonable request of him. Take note of Rehoboam's friendships and attitude toward wisdom in the following account:

Then Jeroboam and the whole assembly of Israel came and spoke to Rehoboam, saying, "Your father made our yoke heavy; now therefore, lighten the burdensome service of your father, and his heavy yoke which he put on us, and we will serve you." So he said to them, "Depart *for* three days, then come back to me." And the people departed. Then King Rehoboam consulted the elders who stood before his father Solomon while he still lived, and he said, "How do you advise *me* to answer these people?" And they spoke to him, saying, "If you will be a servant to these people today, and serve them, and answer them, and speak good words to them, then they will be your servants forever." But he rejected the advice which the elders had given him, and consulted the young men who had grown up with him, who stood before him. And he said to them, "What advice do you give? How should we answer this people who have spoken to me, saying, 'Lighten the yoke which your father put on us'?" Then the young men who had grown up with him spoke to him, saying, "Thus you should speak to this people who have spoken to you, saying, 'Your father made our yoke heavy, but you make *it* lighter on us'—thus you shall say to them: 'My little *finger* shall be thicker than my father's waist! And now, whereas my father put a heavy yoke on you, I will add to your yoke; my father chastised you with whips, but I will chastise you with scourges!'" So Jeroboam and all the people came to Rehoboam the third day, as the king had directed, saying, "Come back to me the third day." Then the king answered the people roughly, and rejected the advice which the elders had given him; and he spoke to them according to the advice of the young men, saying, "My father made your yoke heavy, but I will add to your yoke; my father chastised you with whips, but I will chastise you with scourges."

Don't let the "little finger" and "my father's waist" throw you off. Rehoboam is just saying, in effect, "You thought my father ruled harshly? You haven't seen nothin' yet. I'm going to be 10 times worse." In essence, the older, wiser men counseled Rehoboam that if he'd be a scrvant-leader to his people, they'd gladly submit to his leadership, while the younger, foolish friends counseled him to become a tyrant.

A lot can be learned from the above story about the company you keep, listening to older and wiser people, and seeking out *yes men* for counselors. Let's compare Rehoboam's actions to his father's words of wisdom in Proverbs 13:20. Rehoboam didn't walk with wise men. In fact, he outright rejected their wise counsel. Then he turned to his young, foolish friends whom he grew up with and who offered him foolish counsel. He was a companion of fools, and the result was just as his father Solomon foretold: destruction. If you read the rest of the story (1 Kgs 12:15-24; 2 Chron 11:1-12:16), you'll see that the people responded to Rehoboam's words by rejecting him as their king. He lost the majority of his kingdom, with only two of the 12 tribes of Israel remaining loyal to him. For most of the rest of his life, Rehoboam made foolish decisions, and his life ended in destruction.

It's quite ironic, really. Rehoboam had the wisest man who ever lived for a father and yet he was a great fool. Solomon by no means made all the best decisions in life, but Rehoboam could have—and *should* have—learned from his father and chosen to walk wisely and surround himself with wise people. Instead, he chose poorly, and not only did he, but also his whole kingdom paid dearly for it. Sometime before these events, Solomon bemoaned the fact that after his death, all the wealth he had amassed for his family and for his kingdom would be left to someone (Rehoboam) who he wasn't sure would be wise or foolish. "Then I hated all my labor in which I had toiled under the sun," Solomon complains, "because I must leave it to the man who will come after me. And who knows whether he will be wise or a fool?" (Eccl 2:18-19) Unfortunately for Solomon—and everyone else—Rehoboam was a fool.

Do you want to destroy your life? If your answer is *yes*, then it's quite simple: just be like Rehoboam by rejecting wise counsel and picking foolish people for your friends. If your answer is *no*, then may you not be like Rehoboam, but rather learn from his mistakes.

Be Prideful

Another way that you can express a rejection of wisdom is through having an attitude of pride. In Proverbs 11:2, Solomon declares, "When pride comes, then comes shame; but with the humble *is* wisdom." Notice the contrast between pride and humility and re-member the *compare-and-contrast* pattern of the Book of Proverbs. Pride is the opposite of humility (for more on this, read chapter nine) and, according to this verse, there is wisdom in humility, which implies *what* about pride? There *isn't* wisdom in pride but rather foolishness. Therefore, consider the comparison here: wis-dom is on the side of humility, while foolishness is on the side of pride. And what does pride produce? Shame. Pride produces shame because

1. The opposite of pride is humility, and

2. With humility is wisdom, and

3. The opposite of wisdom is foolishness.

4. Therefore, to be prideful is to forsake wisdom

   and be foolish, and foolishness leads to shame.

So, how is a prideful attitude showing a hatred or rejection of wis-dom? Read the verse again and think of the implications. A person who has a prideful attitude has cast wisdom aside. In fact, the mo-ment a person chooses pride over humility, he abandons wisdom because "with the humble is wisdom." And so often you can see the reality of this as people's pride leads them to do and say things that bring them shame.

Do you want to destroy your life? If *yes*, then it's quite simple, really: just hate wisdom by loving pride. Don't let go of your pride. Don't humble yourself. Instead, consistently live with an attitude of pride.

Foolishness: The Road to Destruction

Solomon tells us that "fools despise wisdom and instruction" (Prov 1:7) and that "fools die for lack of wisdom" (Prov 10:21). Why does a hatred and lack of wisdom destroy a person's life? If the reasons discussed previously in this chapter aren't enough to answer to this question, then let me mention one more important point. If you turn away from and abandon wisdom, the only alternative is to turn to and adopt foolishness. To see how destructive this is, examine the table on pages 18 and 19 which is similar to the table from earlier in the chapter but, whereas the first table examines the *lifestyle* and *choices* of the wise and the fool, this table will examine the *consequences* that each of those lifestyles produce.

It's clear form these verses that by abandoning wisdom, you forsake all of the wonderful blessings that she has to offer and, in its place, you adopt foolishness and all of the terrible consequences that come with it. In addition, Solomon says in Ecclesiastes 2:13-14 and 7:12, "Then I saw that wisdom excels folly as light excels darkness. The wise man's eyes *are* in his head, but the fool walks in darkness…. For wisdom *is* a defense *as* money *is* a defense, but the excellence of knowledge *is that* wisdom gives life to those who have it."

Prescription for Destruction

Let us conclude this section by recalling the consequences of hating wisdom found in Proverbs 1:26-27. Those who reject wisdom will, in turn, receive the following: calamity, terror, destruction, distress, anguish. This is the fate of the man or woman who neglects and rejects wisdom. They may begin experiencing such terrible effects immediately, or it may take a long time to fully experience the consequences of hating wisdom. Nevertheless, they will experience these terrors all the same. Is this what you want for your life? If so, it's simple: just hate wisdom.

Consequences of Wisdom Versus Foolishness

Proverb:	Wisdom:	Foolishness:
3:35 "The wise shall inherit glory, but shame shall be the legacy of fools."	Glory and honor	A legacy of shame
8:35-36 Personified wisdom says, "For whoever finds me finds life, and obtains favor from the LORD; but he who sins against me wrongs his own soul; all those who hate me love death."	Life and favor from God	Death and the ruin of the soul
9:12 NLT "If you become wise, you will be the one to benefit. If you scorn wisdom, you will be the one to suffer."	Benefits	Suffering
10:1 "A wise son makes a glad father, but a foolish son *is* the grief of his mother."	Brings joy to parents	Destroys relationships and causes grief, sorrow, and pain to parents
10:8 ESV "The wise of heart will receive commandments, but a babbling fool will come to ruin."	A teachable attitude and, therefore, success	Ruin
10:14 "Wise *people* store up knowledge, but the mouth of the foolish *is* near destruction."	Gain knowledge	Destruction and disaster

11:29 NET "The one who troubles his family will inherit nothing, and the fool will be a servant to the wise person."	Freedom and success	Loss and waste of potential and, therefore, lack of success
13:20 "He who walks with wise *men* will be wise, but the companion of fools will be destroyed."	Growth and obtain wisdom	Destruction
14:1 "The wise woman builds her house, but the foolish pulls it down with her hands."	A house represents security, shelter, safety, provision. Therefore, these consequences of wisdom.	A ruined, torn down house and life
14:3 NLT "A fool's proud talk becomes a rod that beats him, but the words of the wise keep them safe." (See also 26:3)	Safety and protection	Punishment and painful discipline
28:26 "He who trusts in his own heart is a fool, but whoever walks wisely will be delivered."	Deliverance	Deception and destruction (see Jer. 17:9)

2

THE LIFE-SAVING ALTERNATIVE: LOVE WISDOM

If you want to save yourself from playing the part of the fool and hating wisdom and thereby inviting destruction into your life, then there is hope for you: simply be teachable and listen to the instruction of wisdom. But what is the instruction that wisdom gives? Solomon answers this question: "The fear of the Lord is the instruction of wisdom" (Prov 15:33). In other words, wisdom instructs her listeners to fear God.

Five Key Steps to Getting Wisdom

In this chapter, we'll examine the five keys to obtaining wisdom that are laid out for us in God's Word.

Key #1: The Fear of the Lord

In Job 28:12, Job asks, "But where can wisdom be found? And where *is* the place of understanding?" Job then begins to answer these questions in verses 13-22 by telling us where wisdom *cannot* be found:

> Man does not know its value, nor is it found in the land of the living. The deep says, *"It is* not in me"; and the sea

says, *"It is* not with me."* It cannot be purchased for gold,
nor can silver be weighed *for* its price. It cannot be valued
in the gold of Ophir, in precious onyx or sapphire. Neither
gold nor crystal can equal it, nor can it be exchanged for
jewelry of fine gold. No mention shall be made of coral or
quartz, for the price of wisdom *is* above rubies. The topaz
of Ethiopia cannot equal it, nor can it be valued in pure
gold. From where then does wisdom come? And where *is*
the place of understanding? It is hidden from the eyes of
all living, and concealed from the birds of the air. Destruction and Death say, "We have heard a report about it with
our ears." [emphasis added]

After telling us where wisdom is *not* sourced, Job then proceeds to
tell us that God knows about wisdom: "God understands its way,
and He knows its place. For He looks to the ends of the earth, and
sees under the whole heavens, to establish a weight for the wind,
and apportion the waters by measure. When He made a law for the
rain, and a path for the thunderbolt, then He saw *wisdom* and declared it; He prepared it, indeed, He searched it out" (vv. 23-27).

After all this, Job finally tells us that God reveals where wisdom *is*
found: "And to man He said, 'Behold, the fear of the Lord, that *is*
wisdom, and to depart from evil *is* understanding'" (v. 28). To Job's
two questions of where wisdom comes from and where it can be
found, God answers that the key to obtaining wisdom is fearing
Him. Solomon said something similar: "The fear of the LORD *is*
the beginning of wisdom, and the knowledge of the Holy One *is*
understanding" (Prov 9:10). Where does wisdom begin? With fearing God. Therefore, if a person doesn't fear God, they have no
wisdom—at least, not godly wisdom.

What is the fear of the Lord? The idea isn't that of being constantly
afraid and terrified of God, but to revere and honor Him. The
German theologian, Otto Zockler, said, "The wise man is also the
just, the pious, the upright, the man who walks in the way of truth.

The fear of the Lord, which is the beginning of wisdom, consists in a complete obedience to God."⁴ The fear of the Lord may be defined this way: to reverently believe that God will do what He has said in His Word, and to therefore obey Him. For example, God has said in Galatians 6:7-8, "Do not be deceived, God is not mocked; for whatever a man sows, that he will also reap. For he who sows to his flesh will of the flesh reap corruption, but he who sows to the Spirit will of the Spirit reap everlasting life." As it relates to these verses, the fear of the Lord would be to believe that if you invest your life into sinful things of the flesh, it will destroy you, but if you yield your life to the Holy Spirit, you will experience life. And therefore, that reverent fear—or belief—leads to action: you choose to resist the flesh and to yield to the Spirit. This is what it means to have the fear of the Lord.

What does it look like, on a practical level, to fear the Lord? Solomon furthers describes it for us when he says, "The fear of the LORD is to hate evil" (Prov 8:13). Thus, on a practical level, the fear of the Lord is hating what God hates and loving what God loves. This, according to Solomon, is where wisdom starts.⁵

So, to Job's question about where a person can find wisdom, the answer is *in fearing God*. That's where it all begins. Therefore, as a point of application, strive to grow in your fear of God, and you'll grow in wisdom, guaranteed.

Key #2: Go to the Source

In Colossians 2:3, the apostle Paul tells us that in God the Father and in Jesus Christ "are hidden all the treasures of wisdom and

---

⁴ Otto Zockler as quoted in Frank S. Mead, ed., *12,000 Religious Quotations* (1965; repr., Grand Rapids, MI: Baker Book House, 1989), 469.
⁵ For more passages dealing with the fear of the Lord, see Psalm 25:12-14; 76:7, 11; 89:7; 112:1; 115:11-13; 128:1-4; 145:18-19; Proverbs 1:7; 14:26-27; 15:33; 19:23; 23:17; Ecclesiastes 12:13-14.

knowledge." In other words, wisdom is rooted in God Himself. So, do you want wisdom? If so, then go to God, the source of the greatest treasure horde of wisdom and knowledge. Invest in your relationship with the Lord. (If you currently do not have a personal relationship with God, see Appendix A.) Seek Him diligently. This is one of the primary ways of growing in wisdom. Get to know Jesus more. Spend more time with Him on a daily basis. You grow in your personal relationship with the Lord, and you'll grow in wisdom, guaranteed.

One of the primary ways we can "go to the source" of wisdom is by devoting time every day to studying His Word. The God of all wisdom has revealed Himself and all of the secrets to living wisely within the pages of His Word. Therefore, you must cherish the Word of God. If you don't, you are sure to deprive yourself of wisdom. In Jeremiah 8:9, God says of His people, "Behold, they have rejected the word of the Lord; so what wisdom do they have?" The implication is clear: if you reject the Word of the all-wise God, you reject wisdom itself and become entirely bankrupt of wisdom. There is a direct link between your attitude toward God's Word and whether you possess or lack wisdom. More on that in chapter 11.

Key #3: Ask, and You Shall Receive

The third way to get wisdom is simply to *ask* God for it. Maybe this seems way too simple and that is has to be more complicated. Not so! We're told in James 1:5, "But if any of you lacks wisdom, let him ask of God, who gives to all generously and without reproach, and it will be given to him." (NASB) Wow! That's incredible! God has made it so simple: if you lack and, therefore, need wisdom (and God knows we all need a lot of wisdom pertaining to many things), then just ask Him for it and He will graciously, generously, and joyfully give it to you. What a wonderful promise! One can't help but call to mind Jesus' command, "Ask, and it will be given to you" (Matt 7:7). One of the reasons we oftentimes don't have wisdom is because we fail to ask God for it. James says that you have not because you ask not (Jas 4:2).

But wait! Go back to James 1. There is a condition attached to God giving us wisdom when we ask for it. James adds, "But let him ask in faith, with no doubting, for he who doubts is like a wave of the sea driven and tossed by the wind. For let not that man suppose that he will receive anything from the Lord; he is a double-minded man, unstable in all his ways" (vv. 6-8). James is a straight shooter; he doesn't beat around the bush but just says it like it is. The condition for receiving wisdom when asking for it is that you must ask *in faith*, which makes perfect sense. Think about it: why should we expect that God will give us something that we're asking for if we don't even believe He'll give it to us? By having such faithlessness, we're basically telling God that we don't trust Him or believe that He'll come through on His promise. And if that's our attitude, then why ask in the first place? Therefore, James rightly tells us to ask for wisdom but to do it in faith.

Key #4: Hang Out with Wise People

The fourth key to obtaining wisdom can be found in Proverbs 13:20, where Solomon says, "He who walks with wise men will be wise." You become like the company you keep. Just as it is true that "Bad company corrupts good morals" (1 Cor 15:33 NASB), so the opposite is also true: wise company will have the effect of making you wiser.

It has been said that the best and fastest way to learn a new language is to live in a place where that specific language is the primary spoken language of the culture. If you want to learn German, the quickest and most effective way is to live either in Germany or a primarily German-speaking community, not in Mexico or Australia. The same applies with wisdom: if you want to become wiser, don't surround yourself with a bunch of stupid fools. Rather, surround yourself with a community of people who are wise and God-fearing. Their wisdom will wear off onto you. Now, obviously the implication in this verse is that you not only hang out with wise people, but that you *learn their ways* and *follow their examples.*

A little helpful advice: I have been an avid athlete my entire life. I've played many sports, my primary and favorite sport being soccer. I remember having a coach who would often tell my teammates and I, "If you want to become better soccer players, then you need to always practice with someone better than yourself." There's a lot of wisdom in these words, and the same concept applies to many areas of life, especially that of becoming wiser. If you want to grow in wisdom, spend time with people who are wise, and especially those who are wiser than *you.*

A tip for younger people especially: people who are wiser than you usually—but not always—tend to be older than you and your peers. People older than you tend to have more life experience. They've seen more, learned more, made more mistakes, learned more lessons, and so on. As a result, they tend to know a lot more about life and oftentimes can offer wiser council than some of your younger friends who don't know as much and who haven't experienced as much. The example of Rehoboam mentioned in chapter one is a prime example of older people tending to be much wiser than younger people.

A word of caution is necessary here. Though it is *often*—and possibly even most of the time—true that older people are wiser than younger people, this is *not always* the case.[6] There are plenty of older

---

[6] We must be careful not to commit the logical fallacy known as a hasty generalization which, in this case, is when a person generalizes about an entire group or population of people based on a small sample. For example, it is wrong for an older person to generalize all young people as being disrespectful, reckless rebels because of the disrespectful, reckless actions of a *few*—or even *some*—young people. Even if *some*—or

people who have more foolishness in them than there is water in the ocean, while there are also some young people who are very wise due to the decisions they make and the lifestyles they choose to lead. The Book of Job tells us, "The abundant *in years* may not be wise, nor may elders understand justice" (Job 32:9 NASB). The *New English Translation* reads, "Sometimes the elders are not wise. Sometimes the aged do not understand justice." My point is this: though it *usually* tends to be the case that older people are more mature and wiser than younger people, this is *not always* true. Just because an older person gives you counsel, that doesn't automatically mean it will be *good* advice. Therefore, be careful about who you turn to for counsel, and make sure you always measure people's—no matter their age—counsel by the standard of the Word of God. Even very well-meaning, wise people can be wrong. Therefore, the Word of God, which has stood the test of time and has always proven to be a faithful and true counselor, must be our standard by which we measure all other counsel and advice.

There are some wise words about giving advice in J. R. R. Tolkien's book, *The Lord of the Rings: The Fellowship of the Ring*. The hobbit Frodo is asking counsel of an old, wise elf named Gildor, to which Gildor responds, "Elves seldom give unguarded advice, for advice is a dangerous gift, even from the wise to the wise, and all courses may run ill."[7]

---

maybe even half or most—young people act this way, it's still wrong to generalize about *all* young people and lump them *all* into this category of being disrespectful and rebellious. Now, at the same time it's equally wrong for a younger person to make similar generalizations about all older people as being grouchy, cranky, stubborn people who are stuck in their ways. Though there certainly are *some*—or maybe even half or most—older people who behave this way, it's certainly wrong to lump them *all* into this category and say they're *all* grouchy old cranks because this simply isn't true. Therefore, be very careful not to make hasty generalizations about people.

[7] J. R. R. Tolkien, *The Lord of the Rings: The Fellowship of the Ring* rev. ed. (New York, NY: Houghton Mifflin Company, 1966), 83.

Key #5: Be Teachable

Solomon wisely advised, "Listen to counsel and receive instruction, that you may be wise in your latter days" (Prov 19:20). According to this verse, what is the key to getting wisdom and ensuring that you'll be wise when you're older? Be teachable, and the emphasis in this verse is on the here-and-now with the goal of being wise in the future. Do you want to be wise when you are older? If so, then be wise *now* by being teachable. It takes humility and a soft, open heart and mind to be teachable. Therefore, don't harden your heart when God and others want to teach you wisdom. Recognize that there is so much you have yet to learn, and be teachable when wise instruction is given to you.

A Final Thought

One final warning is in order. There is a time when it's too late to get wisdom. In our main text of Proverbs 1, personified wisdom speaks of the fool who blew her off. "Then they will call on me, but I will not answer; they will seek me diligently, but they will not find me" (v. 28). My warning to you is this: if you keep putting off wisdom until sometime in the future, there will come a day when it will be too late, and that means destruction. Don't wait. Don't put it off. Wisdom is calling out to you *now*. Don't disregard her.

At the Disneyland theme park in Anaheim, California, there's an epic Indiana Jones ride. At the end of the ride, as you walk for several minutes through tunnels to get back out to the park attractions, there is an archway that has a sign with an inscription that all people should heed. It reads, "Real rewards await those who choose wisely." I will close with some wise, beautiful words of Solomon from Proverbs 3:13-24 that coincide perfectly with the inscription on the archway:

Happy *is* the man *who* finds wisdom, and the man *who* gains understanding; for her proceeds *are* better than the profits of silver, and her gain than fine gold. She *is* more precious than rubies, and all the things you may desire cannot compare with her. Length of days *is* in her right hand, in her left hand riches and honor. Her ways *are* ways of pleasantness, and all her paths *are* peace. She *is* a tree of life to those who take hold of her, and happy *are all* who retain her. The LORD by wisdom founded the earth; by understanding He established the heavens; by His knowledge the depths were broken up, and clouds drop down the dew. My son, let them not depart from your eyes—keep sound wisdom and discretion; so they will be life to your soul and grace to your neck. Then you will walk safely in your way, and your foot will not stumble. When you lie down, you will not be afraid; yes, you will lie down and your sleep will be sweet.

Dear reader, be wise! Get wisdom!

3

KILLER COMPLACENCY

For the turning away of the simple will slay them,
And the complacency of fools will destroy them.

Proverbs 1:32

He who keeps the commandment keeps his soul,
But he who is careless of his ways will die.

Proverbs 19:16

The dictionary defines complacency as "being contented to a fault; showing smug or uncritical satisfaction with oneself or one's achievements." Rather than using the word *complacency* in Proverbs 1:32, the *New English Translation* uses the phrase *careless ease*, which helps us pinpoint what is meant by this word *complacency*. Some bad habits that tend to work alongside complacency are *procrastination* and *laziness*. An important point that you should keep in mind is that complacency will often cause you to miss deadlines. Also, a key verse for this chapter is Colossians 3:23 which states, "And whatever you do, do it heartily, as to the Lord and not to men."

The Roots of Complacency

When your car breaks down, the solution is not always to simply throw some gas into the tank. In order to truly fix the car, you must trace the problem back to the *source* of the breakdown. By dealing with the source of the problem, you'll be much more likely to have a good-working car. The same is true with complacency. In order to be more effective in waging war against complacency in our lives, it's important that we first identify what's at the heart of this sin. In other words, what are the roots of complacency? From where does complacency spring forth? What is its source? Let's explore three roots—or sources—of complacency.

Root #1: Pride

Complacency is usually rooted in a prideful over-confidence in yourself. In other words, you think too highly of yourself and your own abilities and achievements. Think of that time in school when you had big assignment due in just a few days. The teacher had repeatedly instructed you not to wait till the last minute to do your assignment, but you were complacent and had a *carless ease* in *putting off* the assignment as you thought, "I'll be fine. I've got plenty of time. I can just bust it out really quick the night before it's due." If you were a student like me who excelled in procrastination, then you probably experienced the same results I often did in scoring poorly on assignments. This kind of complacent attitude can often be sourced in an over-confidence in your own intelligence and abilities, resulting in less-than-ideal outcomes.

Whether it's with school, ministry, work, or tasks at home, a complacent attitude rooted in prideful over-confidence in ourselves will hinder us from doing *excellent* work. Take note of the word *excellent* here because maybe your attitude after hurriedly and sloppily completing a task due to complacency, you think, "Hey, I got the job done. That's all that matters." *Is it, though?* What does God's Word say? It's not merely about finishing the task at hand. It's about excellence. It's about doing a really good job and doing it well with everything you've got, all for the glory of God. As Christians, we should strive for excellence in our work, remembering that we represent the Lord in our work and that we should be doing it all as unto Him. Recall the verse above, where Paul commands that whatever you do, do it heartily, as to the Lord and not to men." Complacency will only hinder you from living this way. Complacency will hinder you from excellence.

Root #2: Self-Centeredness

Complacency can also be sourced in selfishness. We can often be complacent because we're more concerned with fulfilling our own desires and agenda than about doing what needs to be done.

> **Scenario #1**: To use the example of schoolwork again, your important assignment is due soon and you are wisely warned not to procrastinate. You clearly have an important task that needs to be accomplished, but you choose complacency over heeding wise counsel because your priorities are on doing what makes you happy in the moment rather than on being responsible. Your complacency is rooted in a selfish dedication to personal pleasures and to having fun over doing what needs to be done.

When you have a careless ease, rarely will you be considerate of others. In using the scenario above, having an attitude of a complacent, careless ease toward school is showing a lack of consideration and care for (1) those who have helped to put you through school and pay for your education, (2) the hard work and dedication your teacher(s) has put forth to help you learn and grow, (3) the people you can positively influence, help, and teach in the future due to the things you can learn in school *now*, and (4) God, specifically in how He has provided you with the incredible blessing of living in a country where you have the opportunity to go to school and learn.

In the context of complacency, *carelessness exterminates consideration* for others because it places *me* first while placing others somewhere else down the line. Having this type of attitude is totally contrary to the instruction the apostle Paul gives on how Christians ought to live. In Philippians 2:3-4 (NASB), he says, "Do nothing from selfishness or empty conceit, but with humility of mind regard one another as more important than yourselves; do not merely look out for your own personal interests, but also for the interests of others."

> **Scenario #2**: You're at church and you hear a convicting sermon. You know you need to take action in applying the truths of the message to your life (maybe having to do with reading the Bible more consistently, becoming more serious about your relationship with Christ, the need to forsake certain sins, etc.). Instead of taking action and making necessary changes in your life, you choose to put it off and take the complacent route of careless ease and to be a hearer rather than a doer of God's Word. Why? Because your top priority in life is to live however *you* want, to be happy and to have fun. To sum it up, you're self-absorbed.

A complacency sourced in a preoccupied, over-abundant focus on self has devastating consequences, as we will see later in this chapter.

Root #3: Laziness

Laziness can often be at the heart of a complacent attitude. It can also work the other way around: you can lazily refuse to work *because* you have a careless ease.

Scenario: There's things around the house that need to be done. Dirty dishes need to be washed, laundry needs to be done, the yard needs maintenance. Instead of doing these chores, you put them off *because*, in your laziness and tired slothfulness, you refuse to work.

Complacency in Non-Spiritual Matters

There are seemingly endless ways in which we can fall into the trap of complacency, both spiritually and in nonspiritual matters, ranging from the most important issues of life to those of much less importance.

Sunscreen might serve as a helpful example (I'll let you decide where it ranks on the level of importance). Living in sunny San Diego and spending most of my summer days at the beach, I have often adopted a *careless ease* when it comes to putting on sunscreen. I love to lay on the sand and bask in the beautiful sun, relaxing and listening to the waves crash on the shore. There isn't a care in my mind as I take no heed to the warnings from others to apply sunscreen to my baking body. I keep procrastinating and putting off the putting on of sunscreen as I think, "I'm fine. I'll put it on later. I'm not burnt yet. I'll be okay for a little longer. After all, I don't *feel* burnt yet." All the while, I am getting cooked as I'm soaking up that lovely sun.

You'd think that having grown up near the beach and getting sunburnt countless times throughout my life, I would've learned my lesson years ago. Well, some lessons are hard-learned. As good as that sun feels and as happy and carefree as I am *in the moment*, I always pay for it later: my skin turns a lobster-red color and is in screaming pain as it feels like I've been set ablaze; my body temperature, though normal, feels like it is reaching supernova extremes of heat; my heartbeat can be felt in every inch sun-scorched skin; what is usually a nice, hot shower is no longer enjoyable but deplorable; it hurts to sleep because every time I move, the painful sensation on my burning skin returns. Complacency has consequences.

It is very easy to adopt an attitude of complacency toward many of the things that we deal with on a day-to-day basis such as our investment in our relationship with God, our dedication to studying His Word, keeping up on chores or tasks that need to get done, paying bills, eating healthy, and so on. Some of these things are obviously more important than others but, nevertheless, they all have some level of importance. When a task needs to be done but we don't want to do it, the easiest option in the moment is to put it off. However, though complacency is the easier option *in the moment*, it usually comes back to bite us later. It might make your life more enjoyable *now* but in the long run, it makes your life a lot harder and makes a lot more work for you in the future. And remember from chapter one that a wise person doesn't focus just on the now and what will make life enjoyable in the present. Rather, wise people look ahead and prepare for the future. Complacency now will cause you to reap greater, more severe consequences in the future.

When you procrastinate and put things off, you'll oftentimes miss deadlines. As I said before, complacency comes with consequences, even in non-spiritual matters. I used to own a 1989 Honda Civic. I stopped driving it because I inherited a newer 2002 Toyota that ran better. The Honda needed over $900 worth of work done on it and I didn't see any point in spending that kind of money since I didn't drive it anymore. I heard about a company that would buy any car for $1,000 or more if it didn't pass a smog check. I was thrilled! Not only would I save over $900 in repairs on the car, but I'd gain $1,000. Who wouldn't jump at that opportunity? Well, I planned all along on turning in the car, but I kept putting it off and kept putting it off until, three years later, I finally turned the car in and received my $1,000. What were my consequences for my three years of complacency? I was paying the insurance and registration on the Honda, along with some minor repairs, during those three years that I wasn't even using it. After adding up the numbers of all these expenses, I paid around $2,000 in those three years. In the end, my complacency had cost me $3,000 that I could have saved and earned, had I only taken care of the car sooner. What can you learn from my mistake? Don't be complacent, even in the "smaller" issues of life.

Timeliness

Punctuality—being on time—is, to a large degree, a lost virtue today. This is not so much the case in the workplace. Punctuality is still a priority in most workplaces. If an employee consistently shows up late to a job, most likely he/she will be fired. Employers tend to treat punctuality very importantly and are intolerant of employees who are careless about showing up to work on time.

Unfortunately, though most people view punctuality as a high priority when it comes to their job, they do not have the same regard for timeliness in other matters. For example, many churchgoers have a careless ease about whether they show up to service on time. They don't care if they're 5, 10, or 30 minutes late. They'd never even think of being so careless in their punctuality with work but with church it's a whole different story. Having been a pastor for many years, I've seen this all too often. Now, it's one thing to show up late to church here and there because of traffic or unforeseen things that come up. But a consistent complacent attitude of showing up late to church and missing crucial time with the family of God says a lot about where people place church on their list of priorities.

Or, how about punctuality with friends and family? Understandably, most people don't like making plans with a friend to then have that friend bail or change plans on them. We generally don't like having to wait around on people who are late due to carelessness and we feel they're being inconsiderate of us and our time, but then we turn around and show the same inconsideration toward others when we show up late. How lame it is that some people are very conscientious and serious about being on time at work for a boss that they don't even hardly know but they have an inconsiderate attitude of careless ease toward being on time for the people they love most. Are you guilty of being so inconsiderate?

Shamefully, a lot of people are perfectly okay with flippantly giving their word but not keeping it. They make an appointment or date with someone and say they'll be there at a specified time but then they inconsiderately show up late to that event. Timeliness and punctuality are virtues toward which many people today are very careless. They give their word but their own actions prove that they don't even hold their own word and reputation in very high esteem and they don't treat it to be worth very much value. Is this descriptive of your attitude toward timeliness? If so, then that has got to change.

When you say you'll be somewhere at a certain time, do it. This involves giving yourself enough time to get from here to there so that you may show up on time. Therefore, don't do what we're all prone to by complacently telling yourself, "I've got time. I don't need to leave yet. It's okay if I show up a few minutes late." Give yourself ample time so that you ensure your own punctuality. It's better to be early than late. Be a person that everyone can always rely to be on time and true to your word.

School

For any students reading this book, it's common among many students to have a careless ease toward their schoolwork. They lack a sense of seriousness toward the importance of assignments and due dates. In other words, they *procrastinate*.

Having been both a high school teacher and a college professor, there were no shortage of times that I observed this very attitude of complacency in some of my students. It wasn't difficult to distinguish the complacent students from those who were diligent. The complacent ones would typically turn assignments in late (if at all), show very poor effort in their work, and offer *excuses* for their sloppiness and/or lateness. More often than not, the excuses were centered around students apparently not having enough *time* because they were very busy people. (I always found this ironic, especially since many of the most diligent students in the class often had very busy lives as well, being involved in athletics, serving in their churches throughout the week, and so on. Yet, they always found—or rather, *made*—time to complete their assignments and do a good job on them.) Therefore, I would sit down and have a talk with the complacent students and help them realize that the majority of the time, the issue was not that they *didn't have* time, but rather that it was about *how* they *spent* their time. They had a careless ease toward their responsibilities and, as a result, their priorities were all mixed up. Their own enjoyment and pleasure were at the top of their priority list, while completing their schoolwork on time and pursuing excellence was somewhere far below on the list.

Can you relate? If not, good for you. Keep up the good work of being diligent. If you *can* relate to being a complacent student, you can take this next statement as a rebuke and/or an encouragement: you can and need to change. It *is* possible. You *can* do it. But it's *your choice*. Getting into a rut of complacency is dangerous because the more complacent you are, the deeper of a hole you're digging yourself into and the harder it will be to find the motivation to climb your way out. But it *is* possible to get out. With God's help and a lot of hard work and discipline on your part, you can do it. And there's no time like the present.

Throughout my teaching career, I found myself having to teach my students two very profound quotes. The first is from the old evangelist Billy Sunday, who defined an excuse as "the skin of a reason stuffed with a lie."[8] The other quote has often been attributed to the founding father, Benjamin Franklin, who is believed to have said, "He that is good at making excuses is seldom good at anything else."[9] Wise words indeed, and words that pack quite a powerful punch. Learn from them.

Work

The workplace is yet another area in which we can fall into the trap of complacency. For some people, it may be the prospect of simply getting a job to begin with. There are those who put off getting a job because they feel that if they can free load off of their parents and other people, then why not spend their time just having fun and doing whatever they feel like. If I'm describing you, don't think that you can forever take advantage of and live off of the kind generosity of your parents, others, or welfare. I have known some teenagers who, upon graduating high school, continue to live at home (depending on the situation, there's nothing wrong with this), choose not to go to college (or, if they do attend college, they take the minimum number of classes possible and are careless in their studies), and refuse to get a job because they know their parents will let them get away with it and will keep paying all their bills. I have one simple thing to say. There is nothing honorable in this type of lifestyle. Grow up, get a job, and be responsible.

With that being said, I understand that everyone's situation is different. If, for example, you're a *high schooler* reading this book and are an avid student, involved also in other important activities such

---

[8] Billy Sunday as quoted in Warren W. Wiersbe, *Be Skillful: Tapping God's Guidebook to Fulfillment* (Wheaton, IL: Victor Books, 1996), 86.

[9] Benjamin Franklin as quoted in Unknown Author, *Liber Facetiarum: Being a Collection of Curious and Interesting Anecdotes* (Newcastle Upon Tyne, England: Printed by and for D. Akenhead and Sons, 1809), 182.

as athletics, the arts, serving in your church, and have very little free time, then it probably makes sense to not get a job right now since you might become completely overwhelmed and your grades may suffer as a result. However, if you have the *ability* to work and you have the *time* to work (spending all your time on aimless endeavors does not count as being too busy), then you should work. Maybe you're wondering, *Why? Should we just work for the sake of working and so that we never have any free time?* No! There is nothing wrong with free time, in and of itself. Everyone needs it. However, we should work because working helps contribute to society. An even more important reason we should work is because it's one of the reasons God has placed mankind on this earth (Gen 1:26-30; 2:15). More on this in chapter 12. If you're an adult, then it goes without saying that you should have a job. If you can work, you should work. (For the few people reading this book who have more than enough money that they don't need to work, you should still be using your time in the service of the Lord and others.) If you're retired, don't just spend all your free time on yourself. Volunteer to serve in various ministries or other areas to help others. There are all kinds of ways you can be busy serving the Lord.

How different our perspective would be if we viewed work as a blessing and an opportunity to fulfill part of the calling and purpose for which God created us. The apostle Paul has some heavy—but necessary—words for the one who has the ability to work but refuses to do so: "For even when we were with you, we commanded you this: If anyone will not work, neither shall he eat" (2 Thess 3:10). In other words, if a person can and should be working but refuses to do so and, instead, chooses to mooch off of others who *are* working, then people should not feed that person. Why not? He/she needs to learn to work and contribute to society. If people continually feed and provide for those who are lazy and complacent, what will be the result? They'll continue to free-load off of others, and this is not how God created people to live or society to function. Hence, Paul's command. Complacency always comes at a cost—or, at least, it should. Solomon has some words of wisdom on this issue: "A laborer's appetite works on his behalf, for his hunger urges him to work" (Prov 16:26 NET).

Complacency in Spiritual Matters

The Complacent Christian

Complacency may be one of the most dangerous traps into which a Christian can fall. One important thing to note about complacency is that it generally comes with some amount of knowledge attached to it. For example, you *know* that you should obey Christ's commands, but you don't do it. Also, complacency is oftentimes linked to a willful ignorance. For example, you *choose* to remain ignorant of what Christ's commands are because it's *easier* to just live with a careless ease. If you learn and gain knowledge about how God calls you to live, then it will bother your conscience to know that you're not doing what you should, so therefore, you choose to remain ignorant instead.

One of the great temptations for Christians—especially in the Western world—is to live a complacent Christianity, one in which we don't *do* much and in which our level of commitment to Christ is extremely low. In essence, we profess with our mouths to seriously follow Christ but don't display it with our actions. In fact, our lifestyles reveal that we're dedicated more to our own agenda and desires than we are to pleasing Christ.

Complacent Christianity is one in which we have an attitude of careless ease toward the level of our commitment—or the lack thereof—to Christ. We *know* that we need to follow Christ with our entire being, but we simply aren't doing it and we don't really care about it very much, if at all. Why is this so? Generally, it's because we want a comfortable Christianity, one that makes us feel good, one that requires the *bare minimum* of commitment on our part, the least amount of sacrifice, the smallest bits of devotion. As a result, God's accusation against the ancient Israelites becomes true of us, namely, that "these people draw near to Me with their mouths and honor Me with their lips, but have removed their hearts far from Me" (Isa 28:13). Living a complacent Christianity can cause us to become like the soil in Jesus' parable that bore thorns. The Word of God can become choked out of our hearts because we're focused on all the wrong things: the cares of this world, the deceitfulness of riches, the pleasures of life, and the desires for other things (Mark 4:19; Luke 8:14).

What does this comfortable, complacent Christianity look like in our daily living?

Your Walk with Christ

First, we can be complacent as Christians by having an ungodly satisfaction with our amount of spiritual growth and the depth of our relationship with Christ. Generally, it's good and necessary for believers to be content but if there is one thing with which they should never be content it's with how strong and intimate their relationship is with Christ. They should be always yearning for more growth, always seeking to gain a greater love for the Lord, always longing to venture deeper into the heart of God, always hungering to be transformed more into the image of Christ, always striving to press on and go further in the race of the Christian life. And, let's be honest, achieving these goals takes a lot of hard work, dedication, and sacrifice. Therefore, contentment—or more appropriately, complacency—in such areas of the Christian life is ungodly. Have you been living with a careless ease toward the depth of your relationship with the Lord, which is the most important relationship in your life? Have you been striving and yearning to know Him more and to go deeper in your walk with Him?

We are called and commanded by God to be *sold out* for Christ, to be totally committed to Him, to be absolutely surrendered to His will, giving everything in service to Him. Is this too much to ask? Some might say yes, but consider something. In writing to the Christians in Rome, Paul said, "I beseech you therefore, brethren, by the mercies of God, that you present your bodies a living sacrifice, holy, acceptable to God, which is your reasonable service" (Rom 12:1). Think of that picture: a living sacrifice typically was an animal that would be brought to an altar to be slaughtered. Its life would be taken and poured out in service to someone, and Paul tells Christians to live this way toward God. He calls us to present our bodies, our lives, our all to Christ as living sacrifices, ready at all times to be poured out in service to Him. And then, to take his seemingly radical idea a step further, Paul calls such action "reasonable." How in the world is this *reasonable*? Is it really reasonable for God to require such extreme devotion from you? Well, I will help you answer this question by asking you three other questions: (1) who is God? (2) who are you? and (3) what has God done for you?

In answer to the first two questions, God is your Creator and you are His creature. *He* is the One who fashioned and formed you in the womb (Ps 139:13-16). It is *He* who gives breath and life to your body every moment. The prophet Isaiah understood this well when he said, "But now, O LORD, You are our Father; we are the clay, and You our potter; and all we are the work of Your hand" (Isa 64:8). Take careful note of the imagery here. A potter is in complete control of the clay, *not* the other way around. A potter has the *absolute right* to do whatever he pleases with and to his piece of clay. After he fashions his clay into a beautiful pot, whether he chooses to set it up on display or to break it in pieces is totally fine either way. After all, he is its creator and, as its creator, he has the right to do with his own property as he sees fit. Do you get the picture?

God is like a Potter and we are like clay. As our Creator, He has the right to do with us as He sees fit.[10] If God ordained that today should be the day of my death, then He would be in the right in making such a decision, no matter how many plans I have or how great of a future people tell me I have ahead of me. God created me, I belong to Him, and therefore He has the right to do with His handiwork as He sees fit.

Isaiah takes the imagery of the potter and clay further: "Woe to the one who argues with his Maker—one clay pot among many. Does clay say to the one forming it, 'What are you making?' Or does your work say, 'He has no hands'?" (Isa 45:9 HCSB). How ridiculous would it be for a piece of clay to angrily say this to the potter? It wouldn't make any sense because the purpose of the clay's existence is to please the potter. When asking if it's reasonable for God to expect me to be His living sacrifice for His purpose and glory, it's common sense to answer *yes* when considering the fact that we, like clay, exist for the pleasure of God, the Potter (Prov 16:4; Isa 43:7, 21; Rev 4:11).

In answer to the third question regarding what God has done for you, consider the following. God has given life to you. He has given you a body that functions. He has watched over and protected you in countless ways throughout your life, many of which you are unaware. He has made numerous wonderful promises to you in His Word. He has always been faithful to you. Jesus left Heaven, a place of perfect bliss and glory, where the creatures there only ever

---

[10] It is important for the reader to understand an important theological point here. God only ever acts in accordance with His own perfect nature and character. Therefore, He has never and will never do anything that is contrary to His nature and character. For example, because God is a God of truth, He will therefore never lie. In fact, it is impossible for God to lie (Titus 1:2; Heb 6:18). God will only ever do that which is good and true and just because that is who He is. So when I say that God has the right to do with us as He sees fit, understand that whatever God sees fit cannot ever entail doing something wicked or sinful. Whatever God sees fit always aligns with that which is holy and good.

worshiped Him in perfect holiness, and He came down to this planet where His most prized creation constantly rebels against Him and even killed Him. Why did He make such a sacrifice? One of the many reasons was to save you. He has provided payment for your sins by giving His own life in your place. He allowed His own blood to be shed so that you might experience reconciliation with God. He died so that you could live. He has loved you and offered to you the free gift of eternal life with Him in glory. He has been and is immensely patient with you when you repeatedly rebel against His will. These are only a few of the countless things He has done for you, and He didn't have to do any of them. When pondering all that God has done for you, it becomes increasingly obvious that it's reasonable for you to give all of yourself to Him.

So then, in understanding (1) who God is, (2) who I am, and (3) all that He has done for me, it becomes much easier to see why such an extreme devotion to giving myself as a living sacrifice to God is totally reasonable. In fact, it really isn't *extreme* at all. It's normal. It's common sense. It's nothing compared to all that He has done for me. It's obvious that God deserves nothing less than the best, nothing less than my all. Anything less that I offer to Him is thievery. I am withholding from Him what He deserves.

Jesus "died for all, that those who live should live no longer for themselves, but for Him who died for them and rose again" (2 Cor 5:15). Naturally, we live for ourselves, not for God. One of the very reasons Jesus died for you and me is so that we, as a result of His sacrifice, might stop living for ourselves and start living for Him and Him alone! Jesus "gave Himself for us, that He might redeem us from every lawless deed and purify for Himself His own special people, zealous for good works" (Titus 2:14). One of the reasons He has done all these wonderful things for us is so that we will be His own special people who are zealous (intensely enthusiastic) for good works. Therefore, as a point of application, what is your level of commitment to knowing and following Jesus? Are you sold out for Him as a living sacrifice, or do you have an attitude of complacency? Remember that, in a manner of speaking, if you're giving God anything less than your all, then you're robbing Him and living the life of a hypocrite.

Obeying God's Word

Another way in which we can be complacent as Christians is by putting off obedience to God's Word. In a word, we procrastinate. When we study the Bible or when we hear a sermon with convicting biblical truths, we are shown that we need to change our lives. Though we need to have total dependence upon the Lord to help us make the necessary changes in our lives, that doesn't mean that we are free from any personal responsibility. God has given us an amazing thing called *free will*, which means that He won't force us to change. And though He will help us in our growth, we need to make the choice to take active steps toward changing our lives to be more like Christ. A struggle that every Christian faces is being a hearer but not a doer of God's Word, to be complacent toward actually *doing* what we know we should do.

James 1:22-25 tells us, "But be doers of the word, and not hearers only, deceiving yourselves. For if anyone is a hearer of the word and not a doer, he is like a man observing his natural face in a mirror; for he observes himself, goes away, and immediately forgets what kind of man he was. But he who looks into the perfect law of liberty and continues in it, and is not a forgetful hearer but a doer of the work, this one will be blessed in what he does."

Several things to note about these verses: (1) hearing God's Word is good and essential and yet, as important as it is, it's not enough; (2) being only a hearer and not a doer of God's Word is shameful; (3) when we're only hearers but not doers of God's Word, we are self-deceived (and self-deception is the worst kind of deception). We can be self-deceived in a few ways here: first, by believing the lie that being a hearer is enough; second, by telling ourselves that being a hearer alone makes me a true disciple of Christ; third, by being duped into believing the lie that simply hearing and even being convicted by truth will actually change me. Let me explain. Sometimes Christians can hear God's Word through a sermon or their own personal time of reading and then walk away feeling satisfied by how convicting it was, as if conviction alone is sufficient. But a good question to ask is, *Did that conviction lead to anything further? Did it produce repentance, change, and growth?* As the old revival preacher Leonard Ravenhill used to say, it's not enough for you to be challenged, you must be changed.[11]

To expound on James's analogy, imagine you wake up in the morning before going to work, church, school, or anywhere for that matter. You look into the mirror before leaving the house, and you notice several things: your hair looks like a bird's nest, you have massive eye boogers caked into the crevices of your eyelids, you have dried snot coming out of your nose, there's drool dried to your cheek, and then there's some Oreo crumbs on your face from your midnight munchies the night before. In essence, you look like you just got hit by a train. The point is that you *recognize* that some serious changes need to take place. But then, instead of making those changes, you just walk away and immediately forget what you look like. That's pretty embarrassing, to say the least.

Now think of the spiritual application: if you hear God's Word and recognize that you need to change but then do nothing to ensure those changes are made, you're complacent. And in your complacency, you're sending the message that God's Word really isn't all that important and doesn't need to be taken seriously. After all, when we truly believe something to be of utmost importance, it's usually evident by our *actions*. It's utterly foolhardy to treat the holy Word of the living God with such contempt. Therefore, to be

---

[11] Leonard Ravenhill, "Hell No Exits," https://www.youtube.com/watch?v=JZ7xEcFV6po.

nothing more than a hearer of God's Word is to be like King Saul and play the part of the fool (1 Sam 26:21). And think of the ramifications that such an irreverence for God's Word will have on your relationship with the Lord. Do you see the destructiveness of complacency?

Remember that many of Solomon's proverbs are comparing and contrasting various truths about the wise versus the foolish person. With that in mind, let's take a look at Proverbs 19:16. Solomon says, "He who keeps the commandment keeps his soul, but he who is careless of his ways will die." The contrast to keeping God's Word is being careless—complacent—of one's ways. And what is the destructive result? Death. A spirit of indifference toward obedience to God's Word will destroy your life.

Now let's compare a hearer with a doer of God's Word. The doer is a blessed person (Ps 1:1-3; Luke 8:21; 11:28). Solomon again says, "He who heeds the word wisely will find good, and whoever trusts in the LORD, happy is he" (Prov 16:20). In Jesus' parable of the sower and the seed, the fourth soil represents the person who "hears the word and understands it, who indeed *bears fruit* and *produces*: some a hundredfold, some sixty, some thirty" (Matt 13:23 emphasis added). A synonym of bearing fruit in this context can be *obedience*, i.e., being a *doer* of the Word.

The Israelites serve as an excellent example of complacency in hearing, but not doing, God's Word. God repeatedly commanded the Israelites that when they came into the Promised Land and God gave them victory over their enemies, they needed to completely drive out the pagan nations and their evil idolatrous practices from the land (Deut 7:1-5). In the book of Joshua, after they had gained many victories and were getting settled into the Promised Land, it becomes evident that complacency began to settle into the hearts of the Israelites. Note the following verses from Joshua: "As for the Jebusites, the inhabitants of Jerusalem, the children of Judah could not drive them out; but the Jebusites dwell with the children of Judah at Jerusalem to this day" (15:63); "And they did not drive out the Canaanites who dwelt in Gezer; but the Canaanites dwell among the Ephraimites to this day and have become forced laborers" (16:10); "Yet the children of Manasseh could not drive out the inhabitants of those cities, but the Canaanites were deter- mined to dwell in that land. And it happened, when the children of Israel grew strong, that they put the Canaanites to forced labor, but did not utterly drive them out" (17:12-13); "Then Joshua said to the children of Israel: 'How long will you neglect to go and possess the land which the LORD God of your fathers has given you?'" (18:3). Take special note of the word *neglect* that is used in this last passage. The English Standard Version and the New American Standard Bible translate this word as *put off*. The Israelites *knew* what needed to be done and what God required of them, but they were putting off obedience; they had a careless ease, a complacency toward being doers of His Word. And if you keep reading throughout the Old Testament, you'll find that the consequences were devastating, just as Solomon says.

Dealing with Sin

We can often have a very complacent attitude toward fighting against and ridding ourselves of personal sin. If you believe the biblical truth that sin destroys one's life (Rom 6:23; Jas 1:15), then you understand that living continually in any given sin will have devastating consequences upon your life and your relationship with God. At times, it's easy to adopt a complacent attitude of careless ease toward our personal sin because (1) we don't always experi- ence God's judgment immediately after committing that specific sin, or (2) we don't immediately recognize or experience the effects of our sin. Therefore, as a result, we start thinking that either (1) God either doesn't care about our sin or He's somehow okay with it and so we can continue sinning because God's grace and for- giveness will cover it, (2) God doesn't know about our sin, (3) we can get away with our sin, or (4) we are an exception to the biblical truth that sin destroys and, therefore, we don't need to be concerned about our sin having negative effects.

Solomon is a classic example of complacency toward sin. God told him—and every other Israelite king—not to multiply wives, horses, or riches for himself (Deut 17:16-17). Solomon disobeyed all three of these commands (1 Kgs 10:1-11:3) and became a living testament to the truth of the words he penned in Proverbs, namely, that "the complacency of fools will destroy them." Solomon's disobedience and complacency in fighting against his sin ruined his relationship with God (1 Kgs 11:3-13) and he ended up adopting a worldview in which everything is meaningless and hopelessly empty (see the Book of Ecclesiastes).

Beware of having a complacent attitude toward fighting against your sin. In the old story of the boy who cried "Wolf," the boy had a careless ease toward his sin of lying until, one day, it killed him when the wolves came and ate him. Which sins in your personal life have you been complacent in fighting? Answering this question thoroughly may call for some deep digging and serious self-examination. May we be wise and learn from the failures of countless people who have gone before us and from our own past experiences that *complacency kills.*

Reaching the Lost

If you're a Christian reading this book, what is your attitude toward unbelievers, specifically in regard to their eternal future? One of the main reasons God still has Christians on this earth is to make Jesus known to those who are unsaved. It is the call of every Christian to always be ready to share their faith with people (1 Pet 3:15). Do you have an attitude of careless ease toward the state of the lost souls around you who are heading toward a Christ-less eternity, or does your heart break for them? When we are caught up in our own little world and focused only on living for ourselves, it's easy to have little or no concern for the lost. If you are complacent in reaching the lost with the Gospel of Christ, ask God to change your heart. I have often found in my own life that when I am lacking a love for the lost, one of the best ways to restore it is by spending time with them and sharing the Gospel with them. I challenge you to do this!

Standing for Righteousness[12]

It's very common for people—Christians and non-Christians alike—to have a complacent attitude when it comes to taking a stand for what is right. Such complacency can be seen in seemingly endless areas of life. Let's examine just a few.

Abortion may be defined as the intentional taking of the life of an unborn child without moral cause. Abortion is a heinous sin that runs rampant throughout not only the United States, but many countries worldwide. The need has never been greater for people to take a firm stand for the lives of the unborn innocents. Many times throughout Scripture God commands us to stand up for and defend the needy and helpless, those who cannot defend themselves. For example, Proverbs 31:8-9 says, "Open your mouth for the speechless, in the cause of all who are appointed to die. Open your mouth, judge righteously, and plead the cause of the poor and needy." The command couldn't be any clearer. We who have the ability are obligated to stand up and speak out against such injustices as abortion. There are many things that we can do and many

---

[12] Though this category of complacency in standing for righteousness applies to the Christian and non-Christian alike (every person can make a stand for what is morally right), I have decided to group it in with complacency in the Christian life. But let the reader understand that standing for what is right does not apply only to Christians. Every human being has such an obligation.

ways we can stand up for the lives and the rights of the unborn.

Another example includes bullying. As Christians—but also simply as human beings—we have an obligation to stand up for those who are oppressed and mistreated. All the time people get made fun of, picked on, and physically and/or emotionally injured by bullies. And this happens not just at the child level but at the adult level as well. No one likes being bullied, and yet every one of us has probably been bullied in some way, shape, or form.

Jesus' golden rule is to treat others the way you want to be treated (Matt 7:12). You don't like being bullied. You like when people stand up for you when you're getting bullied. Therefore, you and I have an obligation to stand up for those who are bullied, to stand up against bullies, to stand for righteousness. No doubt there have been times when you were bullied and someone else was present who *could have* stood up for you but instead was complacent and just *tolerated* your unfortunate experience. They did nothing to help you. How often do *you* have the opportunity to stand up and help someone who is being bullied? What are you doing about it? Do you, with a careless ease, tolerate others being bullied, or do you do what you wish others would've done for you when you were bullied?

What would the world be like if no one tolerated bullying, if everyone stood up against bullying? Undoubtedly, there would be fewer suicides, less fighting, less wars, less holocausts, less pain.

As one final example, it takes courage and bravery to stand up and defend Christian truths and principles in hostile environments such as a secular school, workplace, or amidst non-Christian friends and relatives. People can attack Christianity and its claims in a wide variety of ways, ranging from attacking the authenticity of our religion as a whole, to attacking the claim that God exists, to attacking the Bible's stance on homosexuality, transgenderism, abortion, and so on. There is no shortage of ways that Christianity and its claims are being attacked by people today. As a direct consequence, those Christians who choose to stand for what they believe will be persecuted. Therefore, a temptation that many Christians face is to compromise their values, close their mouths, and be complacent in standing up for the truth of Christianity and its claims.

Why do we choose to be complacent toward these and/or other important issues? Why do we fail to take a bold stand for righteousness and truth? There can be many reasons, but let me mention just three: selfish laziness, carelessness, and fear. Let's examine each of these a little more thoroughly.

First, we sometimes might be complacent in standing for righteousness because of *selfish laziness*. We know that it's difficult—and requires hard work and diligence—to stand for what is right, but we selfishly and lazily resist doing what we know we should do because we'd rather be comfortable and live for ourselves, regardless of what it is costing others. Consider what our laziness on these issues costs others. Complacency comes at a cost not only to me, but to others as well.

Second, sometimes we fail to stand for righteousness and against wickedness because, in reality, we simply *don't care* enough to do anything about it. Let me explain two ways in which we show our carelessness. First, we *claim* to care but our actions prove otherwise. Think about it: it's generally accepted that people take action on beliefs and convictions that are of great importance to them. We can say all day that we believe strongly in Christian ethics and morals and that issues like abortion or other sins are wrong, but what meaning is there in these proclamations if they aren't supported by action?

> **Scenario**: A pastor slowly and calmly walks up to the pulpit on a Sunday morning and proclaims to his congregants, "I have just been informed that there is a bomb planted somewhere in the building and it will explode in three minutes, killing everyone who is in the building. I genuine-

ly care about the well-being and protection of you all and it is my greatest desire to keep you safe from physical harm. Now, please open your Bibles to James chapter two, and let us begin our study this morning." The pastor then proceeds to preach his Sunday sermon.

Would you believe the pastor's claim that he cares about the people's well-being? Obviously not. Why not? If he really loved his congregants and cared about their physical protection and believed what he said about the bomb threat, then he obviously would have acted on his belief.

If we profess to hold a firm belief and conviction that abortion, bullying, and other injustices are morally wrong but then we don't stand up against them when we have the opportunity, it may be because, when it really comes down to it, we don't actually care *that much*—or at all—about the issue at hand. The Puritan, Nathaniel Ward, rightly said, "Nothing is easier than to tolerate when you do not seriously believe that differences matter."[13] The age-old saying carries a lot of weight here: actions speak louder than words.

The second way we show our carelessness is much more obvious, namely, we straight up say that we don't care. We don't even try to disguise it. We might acknowledge that something is wrong but we admit that we don't care because, after all, it doesn't affect us. Permit me to share a story with you as an example of what I'm saying.

I have had the privilege of visiting the land of Israel many times. Almost every time I have been to this beautiful country, I have made it a priority to visit Yad Vashem, the memorial to the Jewish victims of the Holocaust of World War II. On one of these visits as I was walking through the museum, I noticed a quote that struck

---

[13] Nathaniel Ward as quoted in Peter Marshall and David Manuel, *The Light and the Glory:1492-1793* (Grand Rapids, MI: Revell, 2009), 442.

me profoundly. The quote was from Martin Niemoller, a German Lutheran pastor living in Nazi Germany. In speaking of the Nazis taking people away to be imprisoned, tortured, or murdered, Niemoller said, "First they came for the socialists, and I did not speak out—because I was not a socialist. Then they came for the trade unionists, and I did not speak out— because I was not a trade unionist. Then they came for the Jews, and I did not speak out—because I was not a Jew. Then they came for me—and there was no one left to speak for me."[14] Failure to stand against evil because "it doesn't affect me" is sourced in the most wicked selfishness and in a total lack of care for others. Can you see the destructiveness of complacency?

Third, we sometimes are complacent in standing up for what is right because of *fear*, a fear of what it might cost us. We must recognize the simple reality that doing what is right oftentimes comes at a cost. That is to say, at times we'll receive negative backlash or persecution for doing the right thing. This fear of persecution and opposition can cause us to silently cower when we should boldly stand and speak up. We cowardly choose not to take a bold stand because we're afraid of what people might think of us, say about us, or do to us. This self-centered fear comes naturally to selfish human beings.

In the movie, *The Lord of the Rings: The Fellowship of the Ring*, the hobbit, Frodo, faces a very difficult decision: either to bear the one

---

[14] Martin Niemoller, "Martin Niemoller: 'First They Came For the Socialists…',", Holocaust Encyclopedia, March 30, 2012, accessed April 13, 2020, https://encyclopedia.ushmm.org/content/en/article/martin-niemoeller-first-they-came-for-the-socialists. It should be noted that Niemoller eventually *did* speak out against Hitler and the wicked actions of the Third Reich. He was arrested and imprisoned in concentration camps for the last seven years of the rule of Hitler and the Nazis. He chose to stop being complacent, and it cost him much. However, as I am sure he would agree, the cost of his doing the right thing was far less than the cost of his complacency and silence.

ring and try to destroy it in order to save Middle Earth, or to hand the responsibility of the ring over to someone else. The first option was incredibly dangerous, highly unlikely to be successful, and it would most likely result in Frodo dying a horrible death. The second option would result in a life of peace and careless ease in the beautiful land of the Shire, enjoying all the comforts of home. When contemplating the difficulty of this decision, Frodo says, "I know what I must do, it's just, I'm afraid to do it." Can you relate, at least to the part about knowing that you must do a hard thing but being afraid to do it?

We often put off doing the right thing because it's hard, there's risk involved, and we are fearful because we know that it may cost us our comfort, security, a close relationship, a job, a grade, our physical safety, and possibly even our lives. Such decisions are truly difficult and can be genuinely scary, but ask yourself, *What is it worth to honor men and myself over God?*

Think with an eternal perspective. In 100 years from now when you are dead, you won't stand before men to give an account of what you did on earth. It's before God that you and I must stand one day (2 Cor 5:10). In the end, what will matter more: how much we pleased men or how much we pleased God? Therefore, let us do what we do in this short lifetime for the honor and pleasure of God, not men. Consider the powerful words of Jesus: "And I say to you, My friends, do not be afraid of those who kill the body, and after that have no more that they can do. But I will show you whom you should fear: Fear Him who, after He has killed, has power to cast into hell; yes, I say to you, fear Him!" (Luke 12:4-5)

Going back to Frodo's decision, he chose to embark on the quest to destroy the ring, doing so with great peril to his own life. At one point, he's discouraged and says he wished that he had never received the ring or taken up the quest. His ancient friend Gandalf's reply is profound: "So do all who live to see such times, but that is not for them to decide. All we have to decide is what to do with the time that is given to us."

Doing the right thing usually requires that I die to self. Read again the words of Jesus when He says, "If anyone desires to come after Me, let him deny himself, and take up his cross, and follow Me. For whoever desires to save his life will lose it, but whoever loses his life for My sake will find it. For what profit is it to a man if he gains the whole world, and loses his own soul? Or what will a man give in exchange for his soul?" (Matt 16:24-26).

Doing the right thing and standing up for truth and righteousness comes at a cost, to be sure. But what comes with a greater cost: standing up for what is right, or choosing to cower in silence? Richard Wurmbrand was a pastor in communist Romania at a time when it was very dangerous for Christians to stand boldly for the truth of Christianity. The communist government was pressuring churches to adopt and implement the communist teachings of the state into their church services. A congress was held among the leaders of many different church denominations, and communist dictator Joseph Stalin was chosen to be its president. Thousands of church leaders decided at the meeting to compromise and bend the knee to the communist government. Wurmbrand recalls, "My wife and I were present at this congress. Sabina told me, 'Richard, stand up and wash away this shame from the face of Christ! They are spitting in His face.' I said to her, 'If I do so, you lose your husband.' She replied, 'I don't wish to have a coward as a husband.'"[15] Wurmbrand took a bold stand for Christ that day and in the days following, but it came at a high price. He spent 14 years being tortured in communist prisons and his wife also spent years in prison as well. And yet, if you read Wurmbrand's books, he continually testifies that paying such a price for standing for Christ and righteousness was totally worth it.

---

[15] Richard Wurmbrand, *Tortured for Christ* (Bartlesville, OK: Living Sacrifice Book Company, 1967), 16.

It has been so perfectly stated by Edmund Burke that "the only thing necessary for the triumph of evil is for good men to do nothing." History is littered with examples of this truth. Whether we complacently fail to do right because of laziness, carelessness, selfishness, fear, or some other reason, it's wrong and we need to ask God to change our hearts, that we might take a bold, noble, and courageous stand for truth and righteousness, no matter the cost, as did Jesus and many other men and women who have gone before us.

The Unbeliever

How might the unbelieving non-Christian be complacent in spiritual matters? It's mainly in matters of salvation and future judgment. Many unbelievers today—and throughout history—are putting off the decision to turn to the Lord in repentance and faith. They think, "I've got plenty of time. I'll live how I want to right now and then, when I'm older, I'll give my life to God." Oftentimes this kind of attitude reveals a heart of pride in thinking that they don't really need Christ *that* much. They have no sense of the urgency of their need to turn *from* their sin and turn *to* the Lord *right now*.

The Old Testament prophet Amos warned of this destructive and foolish attitude of putting off the day of God's judgment. He says, "Woe to you who put far off the day of doom" (Amos 6:3), i.e., the coming judgment because of one's sin. Just before this, Amos also rebukes the people for their complacency: "Woe to you who are *at ease* in Zion" (v. 1 emphasis added). The *New International Version* renders this verse, "Woe to you who are complacent in Zion." The Israelites' complacency led them to put off a serious attitude of repentance toward the coming judgment. As a result, they experienced God's judgment. Their complacency led to their destruction.

Imagine the sudden terror of those who put off salvation and, the moment after their death, they wake up to eternal destruction because *they missed the deadline*. Imagine the terror of the sudden realization of those who put off salvation when the Rapture happens one day and they realize they missed the deadline and must face the Great Tribulation.

Jesus once told a parable about a king who invited many people to the wedding of his son. The people didn't listen to or heed the invitation of the king, but "they were indifferent and went away" (Matt 22:5 NET). As a result, these people missed out on the wedding feast and were destroyed by the king. The spiritual meaning of the parable is that the king represents God the Father and the son represents Jesus, while the indifferent people represent those who are invited to partake of the gift of salvation that God freely offers to all, yet they treat such an invitation with a spirit of *indifference*. They don't take God seriously and, as a result, they perish.

What a powerful lesson there is to be learned from complacent procrastination toward salvation. Paul exhorts, "Behold, now is the accepted time; behold, now is the day of salvation" (2 Cor 6:2). Therefore, if you're an unbeliever reading this book, I, along with God and the apostle Paul, plead with you to "be reconciled to God" *today* (2 Cor 5:20). Don't put it off any longer. You have no idea what day will be your last. The complacency of fools will destroy them. Therefore, don't be a fool, but be wise. Repent and turn to Jesus today.

So many people in history have put off turning to the Lord for a later time in life and, sadly, that day never came. They missed the deadline and are now spending eternity paying for it.

Why Does Complacency Destroy?

In answer to this question of why complacency destroys, let's examine the context of Proverbs 1:32. Personified wisdom proclaims future destruction upon the complacent fool. Why? Verses 24-31 explain that the simple, naïve person puts off obtaining and listening to wisdom. Well, as you know, the opposite of wisdom is foolishness, and you can live only so long in foolishness—and thus, without wisdom—before it destroys you. Thus, complacency destroys because it procrastinates in heeding wisdom.

The Old Testament king, Zedekiah, is a testimony to this reality. The prophet Jeremiah had been foretelling God's judgment upon Jerusalem and the Israelites for many years. He declared that the Babylonians would come and destroy Jerusalem. This happened on two separate occasions before Zedekiah even became king. Why is this important? Zedekiah had evidence from the past—two fulfilled prophecies—that Jeremiah was a true prophet and that God will always fulfill His Word. While Zedekiah was king, Jeremiah prophesied that there would be one final time that the Babylonians would attack and completely destroy Jerusalem unless the Israelites repented and surrendered to the invading army. King Zedekiah had heard these prophecies but procrastinated and repeatedly put off the day of doom.

Let's examine two separate conversations between Zedekiah and Jeremiah, both of which were initiated by Zedekiah. By the way, before each conversation, Jeremiah had been in prison for prophesying the truth of Jerusalem's future destruction. In Jeremiah 37:16-17 and 21, we read:

> When Jeremiah entered the dungeon and the cells, and Jeremiah had remained there many days, then Zedekiah the king sent and took him out. The king asked him secretly in his house, and said, "Is there any word from the LORD?" And Jeremiah said, "There is." Then he said, "You shall be delivered into the hand of the king of Babylon!".... Then Zedekiah the king commanded that they should commit Jeremiah to the court of the prison, and that they should

give him daily a piece of bread from the bakers' street, until all the bread in the city was gone. Thus Jeremiah remained in the court of the prison.

This passage reveals that Zedekiah recognized the source of truth: he asks for counsel not from false prophets or false gods, but from Jeremiah and Yahweh. And yet, after hearing truth, how does Zedekiah respond? Does he repent? Does he take heed to God's Word? No! He does nothing. He's complacent.

Let's now examine what happened in the second conversation not long afterward. In Jeremiah 38:14-24 and 28, we read:

> Then Zedekiah the king sent and had Jeremiah the prophet brought to him at the third entrance of the house of the LORD. And the king said to Jeremiah, "I will ask you something. Hide nothing from me." Jeremiah said to Zedekiah, "If I declare it to you, will you not surely put me to death? And if I give you advice, you will not listen to me." So Zedekiah the king swore secretly to Jeremiah, saying, "As the LORD lives, who made our very souls, I will not put you to death, nor will I give you into the hand of these men who seek your life." Then Jeremiah said to Zedekiah, "Thus says the LORD, the God of hosts, the God of Israel: 'If you surely surrender to the king of Babylon's princes, then your soul shall live; this city shall not be burned with fire, and you and your house shall live. But if you do not surrender to the king of Babylon's princes, then this city shall be given into the hand of the Chaldeans; they shall burn it with fire, and you shall not escape from their hand.'" And Zedekiah the king said to Jeremiah, "I am afraid of the Jews who have defected to the Chaldeans, lest they deliver me into their hand, and they abuse me." But Jeremiah said, "They shall not deliver you. Please, obey the voice of the LORD which I speak to you. So it shall be well with you, and your soul shall live. But if you refuse to surrender, this is the word that the LORD has shown me: 'Now behold, all the women who are left in the king of Ju-

dah's house shall be surrendered to the king of Babylon's princes, and those women shall say: "Your close friends have set upon you and prevailed against you; your feet have sunk in the mire, and they have turned away again." So they shall surrender all your wives and children to the Chaldeans. You shall not escape from their hand, but shall be taken by the hand of the king of Babylon. And you shall cause this city to be burned with fire."' Then Zedekiah said to Jeremiah, "Let no one know of these words, and you shall not die." .... Now Jeremiah remained in the court of the prison until the day that Jerusalem was taken. And he was there when Jerusalem was taken.

Once again, in time of trouble, Zedekiah turns to the source that he knows to be true. It is ironic that Zedekiah declared that Yahweh lives and that He "made our very souls," yet he was treating Yahweh's Word so flippantly and living in disobedience to Him. In this final conversation with Jeremiah, Zedekiah is given wise counsel and forewarned of the coming judgment if he disobeys. Does he heed wise counsel? No! He plays the fool and puts off obedience.

In the end, the complacency of this foolish man destroyed him, just as his ancestor, Solomon, forewarned in Proverbs 1:32. After the Babylonians sacked Jerusalem for the third and final time, Zedekiah tried to abandon his people and flee to save his own skin. However, he was captured and this is what happened next: the king of Babylon "made Zedekiah watch as they slaughtered his sons and all the nobles of Judah. Then they gouged out Zedekiah's eyes, bound him in bronze chains, and led him away to Babylon. (Jer 39:6-7 NET). What a tragic end to this man's life. Because of his complacency toward heeding wisdom, he had to watch his own sons be executed, his eyes were ripped out, and he was led away in chains to Babylon to be a captive for the rest of his miserable life. Learn from this man's destructive complacency.

Do you want to destroy your life? If your answer is *yes*, then it's quite simple: just be foolishly complacent in heeding wisdom and wise counsel.

4

THE LIFE-SAVING ALTERNATIVE: DILIGENCE, DISCIPLINE, AND DETERMINATION

If, after reading in the previous chapter about how terribly destructive complacency is, you would like to save yourself from sure and utter destruction, then it's simple: don't be complacent, either spiritually or in matters of everyday life. The opposite of complacency is diligence, which the dictionary defines as "having or showing care and conscientiousness in one's work or duties." This doesn't mean you can't ever relax and have fun, but there is a time and a place for everything, and you must learn to discern when it's time for fun and when it's time to be serious and work hard.

The life-saving alternative to complacency is to take action to have your life characterized by the three D's: diligence, discipline, and determination. In the remainder of this chapter, we'll examine four specific areas of your life that you can put the three D's into practice.

#1: Work Hard

Solomon so wisely stated, "Do you see a man who excels in his work? He will stand before kings; he will not stand before unknown men" (Prov 22:29). It should be true of every Christian that we excel in our work. When you feel like having a complacent attitude in whatever work you're doing, I encourage you to ponder this command that the apostle Paul gives to Christians: "Whatever you do, work at it with all your heart, as working for the Lord, not for human masters" (Col 3:17 NIV). Another translation reads, "Whatever you do, do it from the heart, as something done for the Lord and not for people" (HCSB). Still another translation says, "Whatever you are doing, work at it with enthusiasm, as to the Lord and not for people" (NET).

In everything you do, whether big or small, do it all with enthusiasm and with all your heart. Why should we live this way? Paul answers this question in verse 24: "knowing that from the Lord you will receive the reward of the inheritance; for you serve the Lord Christ." You will stand before the Lord one day and give an account of what you have done on this earth and you'll be rewarded for those things you did for the glory of God. Therefore, give everything you've got as you work, doing it with the mentality of giving God your very best because you want to honor and glorify Him.

I used to be a landscaper for many years and there were many times that I'd become so bored of the monotony of having to do the same old tasks of raking the same pile of leaves every week or having to endlessly pull the weeds to keep the yard nice for a couple of weeks until new weeds took their place. One thing that really helped me to have a better attitude is that I would remind myself of Colossians 3:23 and imagine the yard as if it were the Lord's garden and that He, the King, was coming home soon, and I wanted to make it the best, most beautiful-looking garden that I could possibly make it. Why? For the glory of God.

In the workplace, be the very best employee you can possibly be for the glory of God. If you're in school, be the very best student you can possibly be for the glory of God. As a Christian in your witness to others, strive to represent Christ well in every situation for the glory of God. As a follower of Christ, be diligent in your study of Scripture and in applying its truths for the glory of God.

As you diligently do all these things to the best of your ability, you will honor the Lord and be a powerful witness for Him.

#2: Be Prudent

Another life-saving alternative to complacency is prudence. Prudence can be defined as "acting with or showing care and thought for the future" and "to be cautious." In Ephesians 5:15-16, Paul instructs us, "See then that you walk circumspectly, not as fools but as wise, redeeming the time, because the days are evil." The word *circumspect* carries with it the idea of being *extremely careful* in how one lives. Thus, in essence, what Paul is saying is, "Be so careful how you live." If you want to guard yourself from the destructiveness of complacency, then be prudent and walk circumspectly in life. Meditate long and carefully on the wise advice of Solomon to his son in Proverbs 4:20-27:

> My son, give attention to my words; incline your ear to my sayings. Do not let them depart from your eyes; keep them in the midst of your heart; for they are life to those who find them, and health to all their flesh. Keep your heart with all diligence, for out of it spring the issues of life. Put away from you a deceitful mouth, and put perverse lips far from you. Let your eyes look straight ahead, and your eyelids look right before you. Ponder the path of your feet, and let all your ways be established. Do not turn to the right or the left; remove your foot from evil.

Heed Solomon's wise words here to cast off complacency and put on prudence in diligently keeping yourself in the way of godliness.

#3: Be Busy

One of the greatest ways to combat complacency is to be busy about the Lord's business by seeking first His kingdom and right-eousness (Matt 6:33) and striving to grow daily in your relationship with Him. Growth! Growth! Growth! This is what God desires of you and me. In Hebrews 5:12-14, the author rebukes his readers for their lack of growth:

> For though by this time you ought to be teachers, you need someone to teach you again the first principles of the oracles of God; and you have come to need milk and not solid food. For everyone who partakes only of milk is un-skilled in the word of righteousness, for he is a babe. But solid food belongs to those who are of full age, that is, those who by reason of use have their senses exercised to discern both good and evil.

Just as one feeds a newborn baby only milk because that is all the baby can handle, so also a new Christian needs the milk, spiritually speaking, since he/she is a baby Christian. This milk for the new Christian is good and necessary. However, just as a baby doesn't stay a baby but grows and eventually starts eating meat and foods stronger than milk, so too it should be with the Christian. As the Christian grows, he/she should be transitioning from milk to meat, becoming stronger in his/her walk with the Lord. There is no room for complacency in the Christian life. Growth is essential, and complacency is the enemy of growth.

The author of Hebrews then encourages his readers against com-placency: "For God is not unjust to forget your work and labor of love which you have shown toward His name, in that you have ministered to the saints, and do minister. And we desire that each one of you show the same diligence to the full assurance of hope until the end, that you do not become sluggish, but imitate those who through faith and patience inherit the promises" (Heb 6:10-12). The author urges his readers to press on and be diligently busy about the Lord's business, reminding them that there is great reward in doing so. God help us to do the same.

#4 Be a Doer

One final word of warning. Just as you can hear God's Word or a good sermon and then walk away unchanged, so you can do the same now. After reading this chapter, you may acknowledge that there are sins of which you need to repent and that there are changes you need to make in your life. To acknowledge such things is a great start, but it can't stop there. You have a choice to make. You can choose to go on from here and continue to live in complacency. But I warn you—and more importantly, *God* warns you—it will ruin your life. Flee from complacency. I understand that, at times, this can be very difficult. Complacency is a struggle for all of us. But God has provided us with everything we need to cast off complacency and to live totally sold out for Christ. Consider these encouraging verses.

- "…His divine power has given to us all things that pertain to life and godliness…" (2 Pet 1:3).
- "He who did not spare His own Son, but delivered Him up for us all, how shall He not with Him also freely give us all things?" (Rom 8:32)
- "…with God all things are possible" (Matt 19:26).
- "Now to Him who is able to do exceedingly abundantly above all that we ask or think, according to the power that works in us" (Eph 3:20).

If you are born again then you have God the Holy Spirit dwelling within you, empowering you and providing you with everything you need to live a godly life. Therefore, combat complacency in your life. For, if you don't, it'll bring you down. James warns, "Therefore, to him who knows to do good and does not do it, to him it is sin" (Jas 4:17).

A Final Thought: Combating Complacency

One of the greatest dangers of complacency is that it causes us to lose sight of the fact that we're in a war. This is a spiritual war that is much fiercer than any physical war and where the stakes are much higher. It's a war not between flesh and blood but against spiritual forces over matters of eternity. Every single human being is involved in this war in one of four ways. Either you are:

1. A soldier fighting for God's side and are actively engaged in warfare,
2. A soldier fighting against God's side for the enemy,
3. A POW (prisoner-of-war) who has been taken captive by the enemy and his lies, or
4. A soldier who is on God's side but you're standing complacently on the sidelines, so to speak. You aren't engaged in the battle but you're caught up in the affairs of this life and have forgotten that you're in a war zone.

With this in mind, read the following passages and make a mental note of what they all have in common.

- Ephesians 6:10-13 "Finally, my brethren, be strong in the Lord and in the power of His might. Put on the whole armor of God, that you may be able to stand against the wiles of the devil. For we do not wrestle against flesh and blood, but against principalities, against powers, against the rulers of the darkness of this age, against spiritual *hosts* of wickedness in the heavenly *places*. Therefore take up the whole armor of God, that you may be able to withstand in the evil day, and having done all, to stand."
- 2 Corinthians 10:3-5 (NET) "For though we live as human beings, we do not wage war according to human standards, for the weapons of our warfare are not human weapons, but are made powerful by God for tearing down strong-

holds. We tear down arguments and every arrogant obstacle that is raised up against the knowledge of God, and we take every thought captive to make it obey Christ."

- 2 Timothy 2:3-4 "You therefore must endure hardship as a good soldier of Jesus Christ. No one engaged in warfare entangles himself with the affairs of *this* life, that he may please him who enlisted him as a soldier."

All of these passages have one overarching theme in common, namely, they all say or imply that we're in a serious and intense spiritual war. Why is complacency so dangerous for the Christian? There are many reasons. When we're complacent, we're acting as if the war isn't real or that the war really isn't a big deal and that everything is fine. The complacent Christian has lost the sense of urgency that is vital for the war effort. Peter warns believers, "But the end of all things is at hand; therefore be serious and watchful in your prayers" (1 Pet 4:7). There is no time to be complacent. The end is near, the war is raging, and therefore the Christian must be actively engaged in the battle.

I was in London in the beginning of 2020 and had the opportunity to visit the Churchill War Museum. I was fascinated by an old poster that was used to inspire people during World War II to combat complacency in the war effort. The poster read, "Self-indulgence at this time is helping the enemy!" What a profound point that accurately describes the reality of the spiritual battle. When we, as Christians, are complacent, we're helping the enemy and giving him exactly what he wants. A complacent Christian is no real threat to the Devil or his plans.

Why are you here on earth? What is the purpose of your existence? It is to bring glory to God and to enjoy a beautiful, growing relationship with Him forever. Your mission on this earth is to constantly be growing closer to Christ, to honor Him with your life by obeying His Word, and to be an ambassador for Christ by making Him known to the world. Complacency only hinders us from doing these things. Lately, have you been fulfilling the purpose of your existence, or have you been sidetracked, distracted, complacent?

Remember that diligence is the key to combating complacency. In telling his readers some of the signs of the end of the world, that the coming of Christ will be like a thief in the night, and that the world will be destroyed at the end (2 Pet 3:3-10), Peter then gives a pointed piece of application. He says that in light of all these things, "what manner *of persons* ought you to be in holy conduct and godliness, looking for and hastening the coming of the day of God, because of which the heavens will be dissolved, being on fire, and the elements will melt with fervent heat? Nevertheless we, according to His promise, look for new heavens and a new earth in which righteousness dwells. Therefore, beloved, looking forward to these things, be diligent to be found by Him in peace, without spot and blameless" (2 Pet 3:11-14). Take note of the urgency of Peter's words. We must constantly be looking, watching, diligent, and ready.

In Romans 13:11-14, Paul warns, "And *do* this, knowing the time, that now *it is* high time to awake out of sleep; for now our salvation *is* nearer than when we *first* believed. The night is far spent, the day is at hand. Therefore let us cast off the works of darkness, and let us put on the armor of light. Let us walk properly, as in the day, not in revelry and drunkenness, not in lewdness and lust, not in strife and envy. But put on the Lord Jesus Christ, and make no provision for the flesh, to *fulfill its* lusts." Dear Christian soldier, now is no time to be complacent. We must be living wholly for God's kingdom, busy about His business. Jim Elliot, the missionary who took the Gospel to the head-hunting, cannibalistic tribe of Aucas in Ecuador and was murdered by them, asked God to deliver him from his own complacency, a prayer that we would do well to mimic: "God, I pray Thee, light these idle sticks of my life and may I burn up for Thee. Consume my life, my God, for it is Thine.

I seek not a long life but a full one, like You, Lord Jesus."[16] Shortly after, Jim wrote in his journal, "Am I ignitable? God…, saturate me with the oil of the Spirit that I may be aflame…. Make me Thy fuel, Flame of God."[17]

Remember, Christian, that you're in a war. Now is no time to be complacent. Be vigilant in the war. Do not be entangled with the affairs of this life but be engaged in the battle. It is the 11th hour. Time is short. Life is short. May you use the precious little time that you have on this earth all for the glory of God. Fight the good fight. Give everything you've got. Be sold out for Christ and fully committed to His cause. Remember the words of the missionary C. T. Studd,

Only one life, 'twill soon be past,

Only what's done for Christ will last.[18]

---

[16] Jim Elliot in Elizabeth Elliot, *Shadow of the Almighty: The Life and Testament of Jim Elliot* (New York, NY: Harper & Brothers, 1958), 55.

[17] Ibid., 58-59.

[18] C. T. Studd, "C. T. Studd > Quotes > Quotable Quote," Good-reads.com, accessed March 14, 2017, http://www.goodreads.com/quotes/549103-only-one-life-twill-soon-be-past-only-what-s-done.

5

FATALITY BY SEXUAL IMMORALITY

Immediately he went after her, as an ox goes to the slaughter,
Or as a fool to the correction of the stocks,
Till an arrow struck his liver.
As a bird hastens to the snare,
He did not know it would take his life.

Proverbs 7:22-23

It's the topic that usually has people squirming in their chairs, feeling so awkward; the topic that is usually discussed every now and then at a youth church service or camp and it usually tends to happen that the two genders are split into different areas so that leaders can get down to discussing the nitty-gritty details about...yeah, you guessed it, *sex*—or, at least, some form of sexual behavior.

Unfortunately, in their well-intentioned zeal to keep kids pure, many church and youth leaders have not always taught very accurately on this subject. For example, when I was a teen, I attended a Christian high school and I remember that during many of the mandatory chapel services, we were told things like, "If you have sex with a girl before you're married, she'll get pregnant and then you'll be in a lot of trouble." (I still hear some parents and youth leaders saying this same thing to teens.) This is terrible advice to give for at least two reasons.

First, it's inaccurate. It isn't a fact that every single time a male and female have sex, the girl is guaranteed to get pregnant. More often than not, she won't get pregnant. The problem with feeding kids this false message is that, eventually, they'll more than likely hear about a friend or a peer who *does* have sex that *doesn't* lead to pregnancy. At that point it's easy—and understandably so—for the young person to think, "My parent or youth leaders lied to me about *this*. What *else* are they lying to me about?"

Second, it places pregnancy—an amazing thing that God created—and a little baby in a very bad light, as something that's horrible and more of a problem than a blessing. But the problem is *not* pregnancy. The problem is sexual immorality. Don't bring an innocent baby into this and make *it* appear to be the problem. *Sin* is the problem, not a baby or pregnancy.

The list is too long and tedious for me to mention every way that sex has been mischaracterized and how much bad, unbiblical advice has been given by well-meaning Christians[19] about this topic (to say nothing of what the world teaches about it). Therefore, I'm going to do my best in this chapter to accurately convey to you the biblical truth regarding this issue of sexual immorality. In this chapter we're going to examine several issues: God's view of sex, Solomon's warnings about sexual immorality, and some of its causes.

Distinctions About Sex

A common way that sex is often mis-portrayed to people (especial-

---

[19] It should be noted that we need to remember to show grace to parents and youth leaders who are oftentimes trying their best to do what is right and who have good intentions but still mess up and get things wrong sometimes. This is part of being human, and we must remember that (hopefully) these people are learning and growing. At the same time, we must hold Christian parents, pastors, and youth leaders accountable to the Word of God and measure their advice, teaching, and counsel about sex (and any topic, for that matter) by the divine standard of God's Word.

ly teens) by much of the Church is that it is evil. This is dead wrong. Sex is an amazing, beautiful, good thing that was created and even commanded by God (Gen 1:28). Therefore, in and of itself, sex is not evil but good. As with many things in life, the key is that sex is good *in the proper context.* In other words, sex is good inside the boundaries in which God has created it to be practiced, namely, that of marriage between one man and one woman. Anything outside of those boundaries is sin.

It's crucial for people to understand this because there are many who are raised in the Church who are given this distorted idea that sex, in and of itself, is evil and that you should never do it. Then, when some of these young people who have obediently abstained from sex get married, they often feel ashamed and guilty for having sex with their spouse. They experience serious confusion because they've been told for so long that sex is evil and it should never be desired but now that they're married, they're somehow expected to engage in it and they don't know what to do. The problem is that they were not told the *whole* truth about sex. Yes, a person needs to abstain from sex *while unmarried* and, yes, sex outside of marriage is evil, but sex is a good thing *inside* the marriage covenant.

Making distinctions is important. For example, sexual immorality involves having sex, but having sex is not necessarily sexual immorality. Grasping this distinction is crucial because failing to do so will result in a lot of confusion and misconceptions about God and sex and eventually lead to misinterpretation and misapplication of Scripture. Allow me to expound upon this distinction. It's right for a person to recognize sexual immorality as sex acts carried out in a sinful way, but for a person to automatically equate sex with sexual immorality is not good or accurate because not all sex is immoral, e.g., sex in the marriage covenant. So then, don't think that sex always equals—or is synonymous with—immorality. It's all about context.

Now that this important point has been made, let's move on to what sexual immorality *is*.

Sexual Immorality

There are many forms of sexual immorality[20] but we'll focus on just two of them. *Adultery* is the sin of breaking your marriage covenant vows and having sex with someone other than your spouse. It is unfaithfulness in the *marriage* relationship. Much of the sexual immorality Solomon addresses in Proverbs has to do with adultery. While adultery is sex *outside of*—or, in violation of—marriage, *fornication* is sex *before* marriage. Both acts are sinful (e.g., Matt 5:27-28; 2 Cor 12:21; Gal 5:19; Eph 5:3; Col 3:5) because, as we've already observed, sex is biblically permitted only within the confines of marriage (Heb 13:4).

All forms of sexual immorality entail a physical sexual act. You may object, What about lust or pornography? Though lust and viewing pornography are both immoral and involve something sexual, both of them are sins committed with the eyes and the mind rather than the person physically having sex—though they can lead a person to commit a sexually immoral act. Lust, according to Jesus, is to commit adultery *in your heart*, not with your physical body (Matt 5:27-28). Nevertheless, to spare myself from having to clarify this point over and over again, in this chapter the term *sexual immorality* will encompass not only fornication and adultery but also lust, viewing pornography, and any other sexually involved immoral behavior.

Wise Warnings

Solomon has a lot to say in Proverbs about sexual immorality and its destructive consequences. In each of the following passages that we'll examine, Solomon is warning his son against seduction and

---

[20] For example, homosexuality, bestiality, pederasty, etc.

sexual immorality. One preliminary point of great importance must be mentioned here. Lest any reader naively think that since Solomon is speaking of a woman doing the seducing, women are therefore the dangerous ones to look out for and that men are just poor, innocent victims being hunted by women, remember Solomon's audience. He's speaking to his son (2:1), so it makes sense that he's speaking only of a woman doing the seducing. Nevertheless, men can be—and, all too often, are—just as seductive in trying to lead women down a path of sexual immorality. For most readers this is probably common sense and therefore unnecessary to spend a whole paragraph on clarification, but you'd be surprised at how many churches and Christian parents have so horribly portrayed all young men as innocent victims and all young women as skanky seductresses looking for any opportunity to lead young men astray.

Proverbs 2:10-11, 16-19

Solomon instructs his son:

> [10] When wisdom enters your heart, and knowledge is pleasant to your soul, [11] discretion will preserve you; understanding will keep you, [16] to deliver you from the immoral woman, from the seductress *who* flatters with her words, [17] who forsakes the companion of her youth, and forgets the covenant of her God. [18] For her house leads down to death, and her paths to the dead; [19] none who go to her return, nor do they regain the paths of life.

Allow me to offer a valuable piece of advice to anyone reading this book who is unmarried: avoid a dating or marriage relationship with someone of the opposite sex who fits the description of this seductress. There are several negative qualities about her. First, she flatters her prey. Some men who want a specific woman will flatter the woman as a means of wooing her (some women do the same thing to a specific man they want). Flattery is often an effective tool of deception, and it's a very dangerous game to play.[21]

Second, she is severely lacking in loyalty. Solomon says she forsakes the person to whom she had previously committed herself. The phrase *companion of her youth* implies that she committed herself in marriage to a man when she was younger. Over time, she probably got bored of him and is now looking for something new and fresh. So many people today—both women *and* men—sadly do this same thing. They get bored of their spouse and cast aside their previous promises to be faithful "in sickness and in health, in pov-

---

[21] There is a difference between flattery and giving a compliment to someone. The difference has mostly to do with one's intentions. To compliment someone is not wrong, in and of itself. Complimenting someone with the intention of encouraging, building up, or blessing that person is a good thing as long as it is true and is not meant to cause the person to become prideful and self-focused. Flattery, on the other hand, is always wrong. Solomon commands us to "not associate with one who flatters with his lips" (Prov 20:19). Why so severe of a command to avoid flatterers? Solomon gives us the answer by saying that "a flattering mouth works ruin" (Prov 26:28) and, "A man who flatters his neighbor spreads a net for his feet" (Prov 29:5). By the way, flattery is only ever spoken of negatively in the Bible. Flattery is giving someone excessive, exaggerated, and often insincere praise, usually to further your own agenda or interests. All too often, the motive behind flattery is selfishness. Flattery usually involves the hidden goal of exalting or promoting self. Statements of flattery are, more often than not, untrue. They're deceptive and manipulative. For example, Alexa might flatter her boss, Stephanie, because she wants Stephanie to like her, think better of her, promote her, etc. The motive is selfish as Alexa is giving Stephanie exaggerated, insincere praise for the purpose of furthering her own interests. This happens all the time in politics, in the Church, in the business world, in schools between students and teachers, in relationships, and so on. At other times, the intention behind flattery is to cause someone to fall. For example, John—the flatterer, in this case—knows that by giving Parker such exaggerated praise, Parker will start thinking too highly of himself and will eventually fall. No wonder Solomon says that he who flatters a person spreads a net or trap for that person. Flattery puffs a person up and exalts that person to heights that are unrealistic. When that person falls back down to earth and is hit with reality, it will be quite painful.

erty and in wealth, in the bad that may darken their days and the good that may lighten their ways."

Third, she forgets her commitment to God. Once again, the implication here is that this seductress had at least some form of relationship with and commitment to God in the past. Walking down the path of seduction which leads to sexual immorality causes people to walk away from their commitment to God.

Notice also the terribly destructive consequences of sexual immorality. Where does sexual immorality with a person lead? Solomon says her house leads to death and the paths of the dead. That's not very appealing. In fact, that's horrifying. And Solomon makes the point even more sobering: there's no going back once one has fallen into her snare. None who venture down that road return and fully regain what they once had. The consequences of sin—in this case, sexual immorality—are devastating.

One final point: what does Solomon say will protect his son from the traps and deceitfulness of the seductress and sexual immorality? Four things Solomon mentions at the beginning of the passage: wisdom, knowledge, discretion, and understanding. Wisdom is the key. (It might be good to reread chapter one of this book at some point.)

Proverbs 5:1-20

We will begin with the dangers and consequences (vv. 3-14) of sexual immorality mentioned in this passage and later move on to the antidote (vv. 1-2, 15-20) that protects you from such dangers.

> [3] For the lips of an immoral woman drip honey, and her mouth *is* smoother than oil; [4] but in the end she is bitter as wormwood, sharp as a two-edged sword. [5] Her feet go down to death, her steps lay hold of hell. [6] Lest you ponder *her* path of life—her ways are unstable; you do not

know *them*. *[7]* Therefore hear me now, *my* children, and do not depart from the words of my mouth. [8] Remove your way far from her, and do not go near the door of her house, [9] lest you give your honor to others, and your years to the cruel *one;* [10] lest aliens be filled with your wealth, and your labors *go* to the house of a foreigner; [11] and you mourn at last, when your flesh and your body are consumed, [12] and say: "How I have hated instruction, and my heart despised correction! [13] I have not obeyed the voice of my teachers, nor inclined my ear to those who instructed me! [14] I was on the verge of total ruin, in the midst of the assembly and congregation."

The lips dripping honey and the mouth being smoother than oil reveals that sexual immorality (whether it be the physical act or something like viewing pornography) feels great and seems pleasant in the moment. However, afterward, it brings bitterness and pain. And you can bet that Solomon knew what he was talking about since he certainly had experience in this area, having 700 wives and 300 concubines.

Consider the warnings Solomon gives and the severe consequences he foretells if you don't heed his wise counsel regarding sexual immorality:

- It leads to death and destruction (v. 5).
- It brings instability (v. 6).
- You end up losing your honor and giving it over to others (v. 9).
- You forfeit your life to those who are cruel (v. 9). The *New Living Translation* renders this clause "and will lose to merciless people all you have achieved."
- Strangers will take your strength from you (v. 10). Take note of the way the following translations render the first clause of this verse: "And strangers will be filled with your

strength" (NASB); "lest strangers devour your strength" (NET); "lest strangers take their fill of your strength" (ESV).

- Others will enjoy the benefits of your hard labor (v. 10). Note the following translations of the second clause of this verse: "And your hard-earned goods *will go* to the house of an alien" (NASB); "and your labor benefit another man's house" (NET); "and your hard-earned pay will end up in a foreigner's house" (HCSB).

- You will mourn and groan in anguish that you didn't listen to wise counsel when it was given to you (vv. 11-14). You will have so much pain and regret.

Oh, what tragic consequences come with sexual immorality. One of the many deceptive tactics of sin is that it only ever tells you how much fun it will be. It always fails to warn you of the destruction and pain and regret you'll experience afterward. The importance of verses 12-14 cannot be overstated. Solomon summarizes the realization the person comes to who has ruined his own life through sexual immorality: what led him down such a destructive path was a hatred of wisdom, rebuke, correction, and instruction. He refused to listen to his teachers and to wise counsel.

Don't miss the terrifying words of verse 14. Where was this man when he was on the verge of total ruin? "In the midst of the assembly and congregation." In today's terms, we could say he was right in the church, surrounded by Christians every week. What a warning this should be to us! Just because we go to church and spend time with other Christians, that doesn't mean we're safe from sin and destruction and can let our guard down. Countless people in the Church have fallen into the sin of sexual immorality. We must always be on guard against it or we, too, will fall.

A Case Study: Samson

Possibly the most fitting biblical example of the harsh realities of the above passage is the character Samson, one of Israel's greatest judges and deliverers. (It would be beneficial for you to pause here and read Judges 14-16 before reading further in this chapter.) Samson was used by God to deliver Israel from the oppression of their Philistine enemies. Nothing short of epic stories surround Samson's battles against the Philistines. And yet, he ruined his life by means of compromise and sin.

It all started in Judges 14 with Samson going to a town of his Philistine enemies, seeing a Philistine woman he found attractive, and then demanding that his parents get her for him as a wife. Despite God's strict command that the Israelites were not intermarry with pagan nations such as the Philistines (e.g., Deut 7:3-4), Samson asked for her nonetheless. Samson's parents even told him to choose an Israelite woman instead, but he refused.

Why was Samson insistent on this forbidden woman? He tells his parents that it was because "she pleases me well" (v. 3). The NASB translates this phrase as "she looks good to me." Samson's standard for choosing a wife was not *whatever honors God*; rather, his standard was *whoever looks good to me.*[22] This was the beginning of Samson's fall. He went after a woman that God had forbidden and, to make things worse, his reasoning was nothing but carnal pleasure.

---

[22] Some people may object here and say that though this kind of marriage union between an Israelite and a pagan person was generally forbidden by God, Samson's marriage to the Philistine woman was exceptional and was acceptable in this case since verse four says, "But his father and mother did not know that it was of the Lord—that He was seeking an occasion to move against the Philistines." However, let me explain an important point. Oftentimes throughout Scripture and history, God moved and worked through people *in spite of* their disobedience to Him. God can work and make something good come even from a person's sin, but this doesn't mean that God condones that person's sin. Just because God can work *in spite of it* and can make something good come *from* it, that doesn't mean that a sinful action is therefore acceptable or justifiable. I personally believe this to be the case here with Samson.

Fast forward to chapter 16 of Judges. "Now Samson went to Gaza and saw a harlot there, and went in to her" (v. 1). There are a lot of problems here. First, Gaza was a city of the Philistines who were Samson and Israel's rival enemies. So, we find Samson hanging out in a city in which he has no business spending his time.

Second, and to make things worse, he sees a prostitute and, instead of turning *away*, he turns *to* her and goes in to her. The implication here is not that he merely went into her house and hung out and checked out her home décor and tapestries, but that he had sex with her. When it says in the Old Testament that a man "went in to her," in the Hebrew language this is a euphemism meaning—this might be a bit awkward, especially if you're reading out loud in a group setting—that a man physically went into a woman and had sex with her.[23]

Notice that in both chapter 14:1-3 and here in 16:1 it is Samson's *eyes* that are driving, guiding, and leading him. Samson, though an incredibly strong man who had defeated many Philistine enemies, is enslaved to the lust of his eyes (1 John 2:16). Both passages begin by saying that he *saw* a woman, and this led to him desiring her and going after her. More on this later. As an interesting side note, Samson's eyes, which caused him to sin so often, would one day be gouged out.

Samson then moves on to falling in love—or what he *thought* was love—with a Philistine woman named Delilah (16:4). Maybe there's some divine irony here in the fact that the name Delilah means *lustful*. By the way, it should be noted that though it says Samson loved Delilah, the story never says that she loved him in return. In fact, it seems pretty clear that Delilah didn't truly love Samson since, when the Philistines offered her money to betray him, she wasted no time seeking to ruin his life and betray the secret of his

---

[23] Examples abound. See Genesis 29:23; 30:4; 38:2, 18; Ruth 4:13; 2 Samuel 12:24; Ezekiel 23:44.

strength to the city's leaders.

If you read chapter 16, you'll find that on three different occasions Delilah asked Samson what was the secret of his great strength—the cutting of his hair—and he lied to her each time. In her frustration of being deceived three times (even though she had been doing the same thing to Samson), she says to him, "How can you say, 'I love you,' when your heart *is* not with me?" (Judg 16:15a). One can't help but recognize her blatant hypocrisy here.

Finally, Samson gives in, but only after Delilah drove him crazy: "She nagged him every day and pressured him until he was sick to death of it. Finally he told her his secret" (Judg 16:16-17a NET). So much can be learned from these verses. Delilah wasted no time in taking advantage of his secret. She cut his hair, he lost his strength, she tormented him, and the Philistines overpowered him (vv. 18-19).

The consequences Samson faced for his sin are truly tragic. "The Philistines captured him and gouged out his eyes. They brought him down to Gaza and bound him in bronze chains. He became a grinder in the prison." (v. 21 NET). How sad! And yet, what a lesson there is to be learned here: sin will *blind you*, *bind you*, and *grind you* to nothing. The last thing Samson saw in life was his betrayal by the woman he loved and his own defeat by his enemies. He then spent who knows how long doing the job of an animal, grinding at a millstone in a prison.

So much can be learned from Samson's sad life. By immorally involving himself sexually with Delilah and other godless women, Samson reaped every one of the consequences that Solomon mentions in Proverbs 5:1-20. For example, compare the bullet points on page 80 with the following bullet points:

- He lost all of his honor. Samson gave away his honor to Delilah who cared nothing for it.

- He lost all he had achieved—and much more that he *could have achieved*—to the merciless Philistines who gouged out his eyes and made him a slave in a prison.
- Samson literally gave the secret of his great strength to Delilah and, consequently, he gave over his strength to his Philistine enemies.
- All of the profit and benefit and hard-earned pay from Samson's hard work of grinding in the prison didn't go to him but to foreigners, his Philistine enemies.
- Samson despised wise counsel and rejected the instruction of his parents to marry a fellow Israelite woman (Judg 14:1-3).

What a tragic case we have in Samson. He was the man who *could've* been, the man who *should've* been, and the man who *would've* been, but *never was* all that God wanted him to be. Why not? He compromised, and small compromises always lead to greater ones. Samson played with sin, and sin took everything from him. Oh, may we learn from his mistakes and avoid making them in our own lives.

Now let's turn to examine the antidote that Solomon gives in verses 1-2 and 15-20 to protect us from sexual immorality:

> [1] My son, pay attention to my wisdom; lend your ear to my understanding, [2] that you may preserve discretion, and your lips may keep knowledge.... [15] Drink water from your own cistern, and running water from your own well. [16] Should your fountains be dispersed abroad, streams of water in the streets? [17] Let them be only your own, and not for strangers with you. [18] Let your fountain be blessed, and rejoice with the wife of your youth. [19] As a loving deer and a graceful doe, let her breasts satisfy you at all times; and always be enraptured with her love. [20] For why should you, my son, be enraptured by an immoral woman, and be embraced in the arms of a seductress?

Solomon's antidote to falling into sexual immorality can be summarized in the command to listen to wisdom. In both this passage and the passage from Proverbs 2 discussed earlier, Solomon says that the key to protection and deliverance from sexual immorality is to heed wisdom, which implies that you must be teachable and listen to wise counsel.

The idea behind drinking water from your own well is that you should be content with the spouse God gives to you and that you need to remain faithful to that person rather than "dispersing your fountains abroad"—i.e., going after other people. The point is that you are to share your body and marriage bed with no one but your spouse. We are commanded in this passage to be content and satisfied with the spouse we have and not to be unfaithful to that person. Now, maybe you aren't currently married. So what? Assuming you will marry one day, you are called to show faithfulness to that future spouse—and even more importantly, faithfulness to God—even now by remaining pure and not following the cultural norm of our day to sleep around with whoever you feel like. Even if you never marry, your loyalty is to be first and foremost to the Lord, and He commands you to keep yourself pure from sexual sin.

A Case Study: Solomon

Solomon, a man who definitely didn't heed his own advice from Proverbs 5, certainly knew what he was talking about. (And just because Solomon didn't heed his own wise counsel here, that doesn't make his words any less true.) Remember, Solomon had 700 wives and 300 concubines. He was anything but satisfied with one wife and enraptured with the love of only one woman. In fact, listen to his words in Ecclesiastes 2:10 when in his later life Solomon reminisces on how empty and meaningless his life was when he went after so many women: "Whatever my eyes desired I did not keep from them. I did not withhold my heart from any pleasure." It's probably safe to assume that this included his desire for women.

Solomon committed a similar sin to Samson in that he married pagan women. Those 1,000 women in Solomon's life were not all God-fearing Israelites. First Kings 11:1-2 tells us, "But King Solomon loved many foreign women, as well as the daughter of Pharaoh: women of the Moabites, Ammonites, Edomites, Sidonians, *and* Hittites—from the nations of whom the LORD had said to the children of Israel, 'You shall not intermarry with them, nor they with you. Surely they will turn away your hearts after their gods.' Solomon clung to these in love." The foreign nations mentioned in these verses were pagan nations that worshiped false gods and committed terrible acts of immorality and debauchery.

Solomon's sin in marrying these many pagan women had devastating consequences. Exactly what God foretold ended up happening to Solomon. In 1 Kings 11:3-8 we are told:

> His wives turned away his heart. For it was so, when Solomon was old, that his wives turned his heart after other gods; and his heart was not loyal to the LORD his God, as *was* the heart of his father David. For Solomon went after Ashtoreth the goddess of the Sidonians, and after Milcom the abomination of the Ammonites. Solomon did evil in the sight of the LORD, and did not fully follow the LORD, as *did* his father David. Then Solomon built a high place for Chemosh the abomination of Moab, on the hill that *is* east of Jerusalem, and for Molech the abomination of the people of Ammon. And he did likewise for all his foreign wives, who burned incense and sacrificed to their gods.

Some of the names of the gods mentioned here may not mean anything to you, so let me briefly mention just two of them. Ashtoreth was a fertility goddess that people worshipped by performing all kinds of sexually depraved acts. Molech was the god of child sacrifice. People would burn their children—from infants to toddlers the age of four—alive in a massive oven to Molech.

Solomon, the man who built God's temple in Jerusalem and who was known for his incredible wisdom, disobeyed God's commands[24] regarding women and marriage, and he reaped the exact consequences God foretold: those women turned his heart away from God. By disobeying God, Solomon sacrificed the most precious thing in his life, his relationship with God. His heart was not loyal to God (interestingly, in Proverbs 2:17, Solomon says that this act of disloyalty to God is the behavior of the immoral woman and, now, we see Solomon doing the same)[25] and he ended up worshiping lifeless idols.

The effects of Solomon's immorality consisted not only of his heart unfaithfully forsaking God, but also of inviting God's judgment upon himself. For more on this, you can read 1 Kings 11:9-40. You can also read the Book of Ecclesiastes to get a very descriptive idea of how miserable Solomon's life became as a result of turning away from the Lord. So much can be learned from the mistakes of Solomon, the wisest fool who ever lived.[26]

Proverbs 6:23-35

[23] For the commandment *is* a lamp, and the law a light; reproofs of instruction *are* the way of life, [24] to keep you

---

[24] Solomon not only disobeyed the command to not marry people from the pagan nations. He also disobeyed God's command specifically given to Israelite kings to not multiply wives for themselves (Deut 17:14-17).

[25] There is a good lesson here. In many ways, you become like the person you marry and the people with whom you surround yourself. All the more reason for Christians to be so careful who they date and marry.

[26] This title is taken from Warren Wiersbe's commentary on 1 Kings titled, *Be Responsible*.

from the evil woman, from the flattering tongue of a seductress. [25] Do not lust after her beauty in your heart,
nor let her allure you with her eyelids. [26] For by means
of a harlot a man is reduced to a crust of bread; and an
adulteress will prey upon his precious life. [27] Can a man
take fire to his bosom, and his clothes not be burned? [28]
Can one walk on hot coals, and his feet not be seared? [29]
So *is* he who goes in to his neighbor's wife; whoever
touches her shall not be innocent. [30] *People* do not despise a thief if he steals to satisfy himself when he is starv-
ing. [31] Yet *when* he is found, he must restore sevenfold;
he may have to give up all the substance of his house. [32]
Whoever commits adultery with a woman lacks understanding; he *who* does so destroys his own soul. [33]
Wounds and dishonor he will get, and his reproach will
not be wiped away. [34] For jealousy *is* a husband's fury;
therefore he will not spare in the day of vengeance. [35]
He will accept no recompense, nor will he be appeased
though you give many gifts.

Verse 23 is the key to avoiding all of the following sin, misery, pain,
and regret. The Word of God is a light to guide you in the way of
truth and to rebuke you when you're straying from that way. Cherishing and obeying God's Word will keep you from going down
that destructive road of sexual immorality.

Notice from this passage the long list of devastating effects that
sexual immorality has on a person's life:

- It will bring you down to basically nothing ("a man is reduced to a crust of bread"). It will rob you of so much.
- It will ruin and devour your life ("an adulterous will prey
  upon his precious life").
- It will stain your life ("Can a man take fire into his bosom,
  and his clothes not be burned?"). Just as holding burning
  coals to your chest causes your clothes to be stained,

marred, and ruined, so also will be the life, character, and reputation of the person who commits adultery.

- It will burn you ("Can one walk on hot coals, and his feet not be seared?"). The point here is that just as a person can't walk on burning coals without seriously damaging and scorching their feet, so a person who commits sexual immorality can't do so without experiencing extremely painful consequences.

- It shatters a person's innocence ("whoever touches her shall not be innocent"). This is the work of sin; it destroys innocence, integrity, and purity. Furthermore, several other translations[27] say that whoever touches her "will not go unpunished." A loss of innocence is not all that one experiences, but also sure and certain punishment. Hebrews 13:4b says that "fornicators and adulterers God will judge."

- It destroys a person's soul ("he *who* does so destroys his own soul"). How tragic! Sexual immorality destroys the most valuable thing about a person.

- It inflicts wounds, shame, dishonor, and piercing guilt ("Wounds and dishonor he will get, and his reproach will not be wiped away").

- It causes grief and fury in the lives of the innocent, and it damages relationships between spouses ("For jealousy *is* a husband's fury…").

When considering these devastating consequences of sexual immorality, the words of the apostle Paul ring so true: "Flee sexual immorality. Every sin that a man does is outside the body, but he who commits sexual immorality sins against his own body" (1 Cor 6:18).

Those who say that they can't learn to avoid making certain bad decisions unless they experience those bad things for themselves are foolish. One of the marks of a wise man is that he learns from

---

[27] E.g., NASB, ESV, NIV, NLT, HCSB.

other people's mistakes, not just his own. In other words, he doesn't wait until he himself has fallen into a certain sin to then learn not to do it in the future. Rather, he sees other people make those mistakes, he learns from them, and then wisely avoids those same errors in his own life. Therefore, I exhort you to be wise and let Solomon, the man who experienced a lot of failure in this area of sexual immorality, teach you so that you can wisely avoid these errors and the terrible consequences that come with them.

A Case Study: David

When reading about these effects of adultery, one cannot help but think of the sad case of one of Israel's greatest kings, who was also Solomon's father, King David. David was a very godly man, the writer of most of the Psalms, and the only man in Scripture of whom it is said that he was a man after God's own heart (1 Sam 13:14; Acts 13:22). And yet, there is one particular incident that occurred in his life that had haunting effects on him for the rest of his days. Even to this day, when both Christians and non-Christians hear the name *King David*, they usually think of things like David killing Goliath, David writing the Psalms, and the murderous affair with Bathsheba. (It would be helpful to pause here and read 2 Samuel 11-12.)

In 2 Samuel 11, David's army goes out to battle and he was supposed to accompany them but, instead, he stays home. Therefore, the first thing to take note of is that David isn't where he should to be when this story of adultery begins. Had this one detail never occurred, it's possible that the rest of the story may not have occurred either.

Verse two says that one day David arose from his bed once evening had come (why was he in bed during the day?) and took a stroll on his roof. "And from the roof he *saw* [emphasis added] a woman bathing, and the woman *was* very beautiful to behold" (v. 2b). What should David have done at this point? He *should have* turned his eyes away immediately and run from temptation. Instead, David did a double take and then asked someone for some information about this woman, thus further entertaining ungodly thoughts and fantasies. David found out that Bathsheba was the wife of one of his soldiers, Uriah, who was also one of his friends and one of his elite mighty men. What does David do next?

"Then David sent messengers, and took her; and she came to him, and he lay with her" (v. 4a). David took what was not his and he committed adultery with Bathsheba. This one sin of adultery would lead David to commit many other sins and would be a permanent stain on his record for the rest of his life.

Shortly after their adulterous affair, Bathsheba sent David a message that she was pregnant. David deceitfully scrambled a plan together to cover his sin but the plan failed, so he reverted to sneakily organizing and ordering the murder of Uriah. For many months thereafter, it appeared that David got away with his sin, but chapter 12 reveals that his sin was exposed and devastating consequences followed. Throughout the rest of David's life he experienced many of the effects of adultery that Solomon mentions in Proverbs 6.

This tragic story, this black spot in David's life should serve as a sobering warning to us. If David, being such a godly and righteous man who was so close to God, could fall so hard and so far and was capable of such heinous sins, how much more so you and I?

Proverbs 7:1-27

[1] My son, keep my words, and treasure my commands within you. [2] Keep my commands and live, and my law as the apple of your eye. [3] Bind them on your fingers; write them on the tablet of your heart. [4] Say to wisdom, "You are my sister," and call understanding your nearest kin, [5] that they may keep you from the immoral woman,

from the seductress who flatters with her words. [6] For at the window of my house I looked through my lattice, [7] and saw among the simple, I perceived among the youths, a young man devoid of understanding, [8] passing along the street near her corner; and he took the path to her house [9] in the twilight, in the evening, in the black and dark night. [10] And there a woman met him, with the attire of a harlot, and a crafty heart. [11] She was loud and rebellious, her feet would not stay at home. [12] At times she was outside, at times in the open square, lurking at every corner. [13] So she caught him and kissed him; with an impudent face she said to him: [14] "I have peace offerings with me; today I have paid my vows. [15] So I came out to meet you, diligently to seek your face, and I have found you. [16] I have spread my bed with tapestry, colored coverings of Egyptian linen. [17] I have perfumed my bed with myrrh, aloes, and cinnamon. [18] Come, let us take our fill of love until morning; let us delight ourselves with love. [19] For my husband is not at home; he has gone on a long journey; [20] he has taken a bag of money with him, and will come home on the appointed day." [21] With her enticing speech she caused him to yield, with her flattering lips she seduced him. [22] Immediately he went after her, as an ox goes to the slaughter, or as a fool to the correction of the stocks, [23] till an arrow struck his liver. As a bird hastens to the snare, he did not know it would cost his life. [24] Now therefore, listen to me, my children; pay attention to the words of my mouth: [25] do not let your heart turn aside to her ways, do not stray into her paths; [26] for she has cast down many wounded, and all who were slain by her were strong men. [27] Her house is the way to hell, descending to the chambers of death.

As previously noted, you should avoid people who bear the same characteristics as this immoral woman (vv. 5, 10-21). You should also avoid being the immoral person who seduces others. In addition, you should avoid being simple-minded, naïve, and one who lacks discernment and plays with temptation like the foolish young man in this story (vv. 7-9, 21-22).

Why does Solomon say in verses 1-4 to hold fast to wisdom? Because it will protect you from the immoral person. Solomon both opens and closes this chapter by instructing us to heed his words of wisdom. Doing so will protect you from falling into the trap of sexual immorality. In verse 25, Solomon gives a similar warning to that which he gave in Proverbs 5. He says to stay away from the paths of immorality, to go nowhere near them, and to not entertain those thoughts of temptation even for a moment.

Solomon also says in verse 26 that "she has cast down many wounded, and all who were slain by her were strong *men*." The sin of sexual immorality has conquered countless strong people throughout history (one can't help but think of Samson here). They lacked self-control and self-restraint in this area of sexual immorality and, as a result, some of the greatest conquerors in history have themselves been conquered men. They defeated kingdoms and nations, yet they themselves were defeated by lust and sexual immorality. In Proverbs 25:28, Solomon wisely declares, "Whoever *has* no rule over his own spirit is like a city broken down, without walls."

What were the consequences of this young man's actions of going down the path toward sexual immorality? In a word, it was death ("he did not know it *would cost* his life"). Let those dreadful words sink down into your heart and be a solemn warning to you. The path of sexual immorality leads one to destruction. As Solomon says, the house of sexual immorality "is the way to hell, descending to the chambers of death." Let's now explore some warning signs to gauge whether we're heading down that perilous path.

The Road to Sexual Immorality

What are the causes of sexual immorality? What are the earmarks—

or identifying features—that lead a person to commit sexual immorality? Identifying these earmarks will help us to detect them in our own lives and to avoid them in the future. As Solomon says more than once, "A prudent *man* foresees evil *and* hides himself" (Prov 22:3; 27:12). In order to hide ourselves from the evil of immorality in the future, we must learn to foresee it coming while it is still in the distance. And in order to do this, we must learn to detect and discern the warning signs before it's too late. It is to this task that we now turn. Let's examine five key factors that play a pivotal role in leading a person down the road to sexual immorality.

The Heart of the Problem

It's important to begin with the core issue. The heart of the problem is the heart. The source of this problem of sexual immorality is mankind's wicked heart. Jeremiah 17:9 says, "The heart *is* deceitful above all *things, a*nd desperately wicked; who can know it?" It goes without saying that if something is deceitful, then it isn't trustworthy. Therefore, if our heart is the most deceitful thing out there then we shouldn't naïvely trust and follow it—at least, not if we want to believe and follow the truth. Yet this is exactly what our culture foolishly preaches and promotes. It tells you to listen to your heart, trust your heart, follow your heart. I say yes, follow your heart if you want to be terribly deceived and go down a road to destruction. Why would a person trust in something that's incredibly deceitful and desperately wicked? To do so is madness and folly. Solomon himself said, "He who trusts in his own heart is a fool" (Prov 28:26). This verse goes to show just how contrary the world's advice is to God's Word.

So, what does the heart have to do with sexual immorality? Well, long before the physical acts of fornication or adultery are carried out, they begin in a person's heart. The words of Jesus make this point clear. "But those things which proceed out of the mouth come from the heart, and they defile a man. For out of the heart proceed evil thoughts, murders, adulteries, fornications, thefts, false witness, blasphemies" (Matt 15:18-19). These seven sins (not an all-inclusive list) begin in one's heart before they are acted upon physically—or outwardly. Therefore, the first step down the road to destructive sexual immorality is to entertain unbiblical sexual ideas *in the heart*. Furthermore, Jesus also said in the Sermon on the Mount, "You have heard that it was said to those of old, *'You shall not commit adultery.'* But I say to you that whoever looks at a woman to lust for her has already committed adultery with her in his heart" (Matt 5:27-28). The point is that the heart is where it all begins. It's not only the physical act that is sinful; the beginning of the act in the heart is also sin.

Now that we've detected the root of the problem, what can we do about it? Solomon gives us wise counsel. "Keep your heart with all diligence, for out of it *spring* the issues of life" (Prov 4:23). Other translations say, "Guard your heart" (NET, NIV, NLT) or "Watch over your heart" (NASB). In other words, guard what comes in and guard what comes out of your heart. You are the one who controls the inflow and outflow of your heart. We must be so careful what we allow into our hearts because what begins in the heart will eventually make its way back out in either a beautiful or terrible form. You are not a robot. God created you with free will and, though you need His help to guard your heart, you are the one who is responsible for the purity or pollution of your heart.

Solomon also commanded his son to "guide your heart in the way" (Prov 23:19). What does this mean? Rather than let your *heart* lead *you, you* need to lead your *heart*. Guide it in the ways of truth and righteousness. Constantly fill it with good things rather than perversions. Do as David did and hide God's Word in your heart (Ps 119:11). Notice David's purpose in doing this: "that I might not sin against You." Filling your heart with the truth of God's Word is a powerful deterrent to sin. Remember, your heart is deceitful. Therefore, guide it by filling it with truth. This will help conform your heart to the ways of God.

Lust

What is *lust?* Though it is most often used by people today when speaking specifically of immoral *sexual* desire, lust is much broader than that. Lust is simply *any* evil desire, sexual or non-sexual. Nevertheless, in the context of this chapter, we'll refer to lust only as it pertains to sexually immoral desire. To lust after someone is to have immoral sexual desire for that person that is outside of God's boundaries.

Recall the words of Jesus mentioned earlier from the Sermon on the Mount: "You have heard that it was said to those of old, *'You shall not commit adultery.'* But I say to you that whoever looks at a woman to lust for her has already committed adultery with her in his heart." The key components of lust are your eyes and your heart. Lust is a key factor that leads one down the road to sexual immorality. And, as Jesus clearly conveys, it isn't only the physical act of sexual immorality that is displeasing to God, it's also the lust that takes place in one's heart. While humans tend to look only at the outward actions, God looks at the heart and, by His standard, lust is sexual immorality taking place in the heart.

The Mind: The Fantasizing Warzone

Imagine that a machine existed in the form of a helmet with a large screen on top that faced outward in front of you. This machine reads every single thought that you have and then broadcasts it on the screen to everyone around you. They can read or see everything you're thinking. Would you wear the helmet? I think it goes without saying that no one in their right mind would want to wear that helmet because they don't want people knowing a lot of what they're thinking about 24/7. The reason is because they'd be so embarrassed and humiliated if everyone could see and read the content of their thoughts and fantasies and what is going on in their mind.

The mind is a warzone of sinful fantasy. Once a tiny seed of a lustful thought is planted in the mind, it's so easy to let that thought run wild and free down a trail of sin that breaks off into endless other sinful paths. It's like a root of a weed that splits off into so many different veins and leads down so many other dangerous paths. You know what I mean. You know what it's like when a little lustful thought pops into your head and you let your mind wander down dangerous roads and, before you know it, your mind is polluted with the sewage of sin. You stop and wonder, "Where did that come from? How did that even happen?" Your mind just takes off with one little sinful idea and, in such a short time, it takes you so many places you have no business exploring.

Now let me make one important point about both the heart and the mind. Though the heart and mind may be two of the most common places sin occurs, this is *not* how God created them. God created the heart and mind as beautiful things to be used for His glory, and they still can be. But if we're going to be honest, we probably use them more for sin than for God's glory. The mind, though a beautiful thing created by God, can be—and all too often *is*—used for so much evil.

Now that we've detected the destructive tendencies of the mind, what can we do to change it? As with the heart, so with the mind: we must be diligent to guard it. With all the evil that the world, our flesh, and the Devil want to plant in our minds, no wonder God gave the Christian a "helmet of salvation" (Eph 6:17) to guard and protect our minds.

The apostle Paul gives us profound encouragement and wise instruction in 2 Corinthians 10:4-6. "For the weapons of our warfare *are* not carnal but mighty in God for pulling down strongholds, casting down arguments and every high thing that exalts itself against the knowledge of God, bringing every thought into captivity to the obedience of Christ, and being ready to punish all disobedience." First, the encouragement: God has equipped the Christian with effective, powerful weapons to tear down and destroy evil strongholds, and we need to take advantage of those weapons and use them for God's glory to walk in triumph over sin. Be encouraged. You *can* do it through the Lord's power. Therefore, look to Christ for help. Ask the Spirit for strength to deny the flesh.

Second, what do we do about the mind? As Paul said, you need to take every sinful thought captive to obeying Jesus. When you recognize that you're having lustful thoughts, don't continue down that fantasizing road but take those thoughts captive and turn your attention to the things of God. In Colossians 3:2, Paul commands, "Set your mind on things above, not on things on the earth." This is your choice. While we need God's help to obey this command, we must make the choice to ask Him for help and then take action by actively and intentionally turning our mind away from immoral thoughts and meditating on the things of God.

The Eyes

Jesus said, "The lamp of the body is the eye" (Luke 11:34; Matt 6:22). Ponder these powerful words. That which you allow your eyes to see will make its way down into your heart and permeate your entire life. Who knew that your eyes have such a powerful influence over your life! Furthermore, Jesus declared, "Therefore, when your eye is good, your whole body also is full of light. But when *your eye* is bad, your body also *is* full of darkness" (Luke 11:34). Who knew that your eyes are the doorway through which endless light or darkness can fill your life! No wonder Jesus then gave this sobering, imperative warning, "Therefore take heed that the light which is in you is not darkness" (Luke 11:35).

A lesson from the kitchen is in order. Leaven. When you place just a tiny pinch of it into a huge lump of dough, it causes the dough to rise so that you end up with a good, poofy loaf of bread. That tiny little bit of leaven permeates—or spreads throughout—the entire lump of dough and totally changes its outcome. Leaven is often-times used in Scripture as an illustration of the effects of sin. Just a little bit of sin can permeate so much of your life and cause insur-mountable damage. What you allow your eyes to see is a lot like leaven. It will infiltrate your life, your heart, your mind, your soul. Do you see, then, why it is of utmost importance that we vigorous-ly guard our eyes from impurity? May we have the testimony of Job who said, "I made a covenant with my eyes not to look with lust at a young woman" (Job 31:1 NLT).

The Love Killer: Porn

Never before in the history of the world has the obtainment of pornography been easier than it is today. Obtaining pornography used to be a relatively difficult—and even a shameful and secret—pursuit. However, with the boom in modern technology and easy access to the internet, we have countless opportunities to view porn right at the tips of our fingers through the avenues of smart phones, computers, and nudity portrayed on the tv screen in count-less movies and TV shows.

We live in a culture that deifies and worships sex. It seems that al-most everywhere we turn, we are bombarded in some way, shape, or form with images and ideas relating to sex. From billboards to TV commercials to sexual innuendoes in films to sex scenes in movies to explicit lyrics in songs to what people post on social me-dia, there is a constant promotion of sex in our culture. There is such an inordinate obsession with sex. It's one of the many idols of our nation—and many other nations—today. No wonder, then, that pornography has become one of the largest money-making industries in the world.

Pornography addiction is a sin to which no shortage of people are enslaved. Let me also mention an important point here that often is overlooked in the Church. It isn't just males that struggle with porn addiction; there are also many females who suffer from this addiction as well. In my many years of youth ministry, I have heard numerous stories of young women who felt so horrible and that there was something abnormally wrong with them because they struggled with pornography but they were repeatedly told in church that porn addiction is only a problem that males face. Unfortunately, this incorrect teaching in many churches has done terrible damage.

Here are just a few statistics that have been polled regarding the increasing rate of female pornography usage. Covenant Eyes, an organization dedicated to helping people experience victory over porn addiction, found in one study that 32% of female students viewed pornography for the first time before they were teenagers.[28] Another study estimated that 76% of females between the ages of 18 and 30 view pornography on a monthly basis[29] and that "25% of married females reportedly access pornography"[30] monthly. And the list goes on.

As a result of being taught that porn addiction is only "a guy's problem," many young women in the Church feel that they can't be transparent with their parents or leaders and confess that they have a porn addiction because they'll be viewed as some abnormal, strange case. But female porn addiction is *not* a strange case but rather a growing reality. Therefore, I urge church leaders to stop speaking of porn addiction as if it were solely a male problem and speak of it as it is in truth, that though it generally may be more

---

[28] Covenant Eyes, "Pornography Statistics," CovenantEyes.com, accessed November 10, 2020, https://www.covenanteyes.com/pornstats/.

[29] See Lauren Brande, "Women with Porn Addictions," American Addiction Centers, August 23, 2020, accessed November 11, 2020, https://www.projectknow.com/porn-addiction/women/. It should be noted that I do not agree with everything Brande says in this article, such as her claim that viewing pornography can have positive effects.

[30] Alexander Blaszczynski, "Excessive Pornography Use: Empirically-Enhanced Treatment Interventions," *Australian Clinical Psychologist* 2, no. 1 (2016): 3. See also,

prevalent among males, it certainly isn't a "males only" problem.

Many people, both inside and outside of the Church, believe that viewing pornography has generally harmless effects. However, this is far from the truth. Let's examine just four of the many terrible effects of pornography.

Abuse, Prostitution, and Trafficking of Workers

For one thing, there have been many people in the porn industry who have been forced to commit sex acts against their own will. There are testimonies from many people formerly involved in the porn industry who have said that they were coerced and forced against their will to perform many sex acts with which they were uncomfortable and, when they tried to voice their concerns and reservations, they were threatened.[31] Furthermore, there is overwhelming evidence that much of the pornography that exists has been created via people who are sex trafficked.[32] Pastor and author David Platt states, "Research continually demonstrates a clear link between sex trafficking and the production of pornography."[33] What logical connection, then, can we make between such atrocious realities and the viewing of pornography? Platt again rightly

---

[31] See Pornography + Sex Trafficking, https://stoptraffickingdemand.com/about/. Click on the following tabs for testimonies of forced coercion and violence done to people in the porn industry: "Stories" and "Resources." See also, "Performers Are Sometimes Forced or Coerced During the Production of Mainstream Pornography," Pornography + Sex Trafficking, https://stoptraffickingdemand.com/trafficking-within-the-industry/. See also, "Forced Sex Acts Between A Trafficked Woman or Child and A 'John' Are Often Filmed and Photographed," Pornography + Sex Trafficking, https://stoptraffickingdemand.com/forced-acts-recorded/.

[32] See https://stoptraffickingdemand.com/resources/ for many articles, papers, and videos documenting the reality of the role that sex trafficking plays in the porn industry.

[33] David Platt, *A Compassionate Call to Counter-Culture* (Carol Stream, IL: Tyndale House Publishers, 2015), 123.

says, "Men and women who indulge in pornography are creating the demand for more prostitutes, and in turn they are fueling the sex-trafficking industry."[34]

Dehumanization

Second, viewing pornography isn't a harmless activity because it objectifies human beings. In other words, it devalues a human being who is created in the image of God and who has intrinsic meaning and value and worth, and it degrades that person to the level of being a mere object to be used for someone else's pleasure. To the eyes of the viewer, pornography transforms a person on the screen from a precious human created in God's image to nothing but an object existing solely to gratify one's lust. Pornography dehumanizes and brings a person down to the level of being nothing more than a piece of meat that exists for no other reason than to fulfill the indulgent pleasures and fantasies of the viewer. This is *not* how God created human beings to be viewed by their fellow humans. Rather, it is exactly how Satan wants people to view other human beings.

God created us to love, cherish, value, and respect one another, and pornography so brainwashes a person from exhibiting such attitudes toward people. In fact, Jesus said that God's second greatest commandment to mankind is to "love your neighbor as yourself" (Matt 22:39). We cannot do this fully if we don't see people the way God sees them. Viewing pornography makes it virtually impossible to see the people on the screen the way God sees them, not to mention how it will affect the way you'll start viewing other people as well. In other words, it's not only people on the screen that you'll objectify and dehumanize, but you'll start doing the same to people you see on a day-to-day basis as well, thinking of them in sexually immoral contexts and fantasizing about their bod-

---

[34] Ibid., 123.

ies. Thus, viewing pornography will keep you from obeying one of the most important commandments of God.

Pornography kills true, biblical love, and not only as it pertains to loving the people on the screen the way God loves them. Porn also has detrimental effects on love because it damages the viewer's relationship with their significant other, whether in marriage, engagement, or a dating relationship. Like termites eating through and eroding the strength of wood, or like rust corroding metal, so porn erodes the viewer's love for their significant other. When looking at porn, the viewer brings another person—or rather other *people*—into a relationship that is supposed to consist of only him/her and his/her partner.[35] By doing this, people who view porn are, in reality, exhibiting discontentment with their significant other and are, in essence, saying he or she isn't enough. And such actions and attitudes have tragic effects on their partner.

Ponder the following heart-breaking words from a woman named Katie G. whose husband has been a porn addict for decades. While engaged, her fiancée (now husband) told her of his addiction, and it devastated her:

> The sacredness I had imagined for our wedding night, the intimacy which we would share, was destroyed. How many women had he already had sex with in his mind? How many perfectly luscious breasts, chiseled abs, and plump buttocks would he compare me to, in this, my moment of ultimate vulnerability? Would he, could he love me, when for him, his history of intimacy was entirely selfish, and removed from any kind, selfless emotion? How could he love me, when the very sight of me might trigger a

---

[35] I am using the term *partner* not in the way that some people use it when referring to homosexual relationships but rather to a relationship between a man and a woman.

memory of porn?[36]

Pornography has truly tragic and devastating effects on relationships. There are so many other testimonies from people who have had similar tragic experiences.[37] The porn viewer's significant other is often left feeling like they aren't enough, they're ugly, they're undesirable since their lover is going to strangers for fulfilling pleasure, and so on. The significant other also frequently experiences misplaced guilt, shame, humiliation, embarrassment, and more. The reason for this is because the significant other feels that they themself have done something wrong—which is why I say their guilt is misplaced—when, in reality, the real problem is with their lover's unfaithfulness. Porn destroys true love. More on this shortly.

Illusions

A third harmful effect of pornography is that it distorts and misrepresents reality. A typical routine in the pornographic industry is that actors and actresses will spend hours before a set or shoot being caked with makeup, thus covering up any and all bodily flaws so as to appear perfect on the screen. Furthermore, it's amazing how the photoshop tool will cover up all the stretch marks, acne, and any other unwanted features, and it will also deceptively increase the size of certain body parts while decreasing the amount of one's body fat, wrinkles, and other realities that people find unat-

---

[36] Katie G., "100+ Personal Stories Of Harm Or Negative Effects by Pornography, Prostitution, Stripping, Sexual Slavery, Sex Trafficking, Sexual Harassment, Sexual Abuse, Our Pornified Society, etc.," AntiPornography.org, accessed August 6, 2020, https://www.antipornography.org/harm_stories.html#171863. Scroll down the page until you come to the story titled, "Katie G. (Husband's porn addiction devastated her life) (female, 25, Utah, Social Worker) (Sept. 9, 2014) PORN – TOO CLOSE TO HOME."

[37] Ibid., https://www.antipornography.org/harm_stories.html#171863.

tractive. My point is that the screen doesn't portray these people as they are in truth. It provides the viewer with a distorted view of reality. In essence, it causes the viewer to be duped into believing the lie that the way people appear on the screen is an accurate representation of reality—or, at least, that it accurately portrays how people are *supposed to* look. In reality, though, what the screen portrays is a terrible illusion with devastating effects. This has a profoundly tragic impact upon a person's life, which is discussed in the next harmful effect of pornography.

Porn Ruins Relationships

The anti-porn organization, Fight the New Drug, put out a t-shirt a while back with a very strong and appropriate message. In big letters across the shirt is the message "PORN KILLS LOVE." As viewers of pornography become brainwashed into thinking that the naked bodies displayed on the screen are an accurate portrayal of reality, they can—and often do—experience a shocking wakeup call when they have sex with another person (this happens to people both in the marriage relationship and to people who have sex before marriage). What they find shocking is that the person with whom they have sex and whom they see naked for the first time doesn't live up to the unrealistic expectations they had of how he/she would look. And where did they get such outlandish, unrealistic expectations and standards? From the deceptive porn displayed on their phone, computer, or TV screen.

The tragic result is that these porn viewers then tend to become disgusted by, resentful toward, and turned off by their own spouse because they've been duped into believing the unrealistic, deceptive presentations of pornography while all along their spouse represents the true version of reality. Viewers of porn cause serious damage to one of the most important relationships of their lives. And to any unmarried readers, don't be deceived into thinking that it's only *married* viewers of pornography who cause such damage.

Porn viewers who are *not yet married* are also setting themselves up for serious problems in their future marriage relationship. The pornographic images one sees stays with that person for a very long time. Even if a person hasn't viewed porn in, say, a few years before they get married, many of those images are still there, locked away in the brain's memory bank, when they enter the marriage covenant. Therefore, viewing pornography *now* causes not only *present* damage to your own personal life, but it also has *future* effects to your marriage relationship that hasn't even begun yet.

Self-deception is oftentimes the worst kind of deception. Consider the following ways self-deception can manifest itself in the context of viewing porn: telling yourself you're just going to click on a site but not really look at the content; telling yourself that you'll explore a bit and get *close* to the boundary line but that you won't actually *cross* it; telling yourself that you won't give in *this time* as you toy with temptation and get closer and closer to sin. And what happens? You give in. You cross the line. You fall.

Your sinful flesh knows no limits. You give it an inch, and it'll take a mile. This is why you must heed the exhortation of Paul when he says to "make no provision for the flesh, to *fulfill its* lusts" (Rom 13:14). Recall the instruction of Solomon from Proverbs 5:8 regarding the seductress: "Remove your way far from her, and do not go near the door of her house." Figuratively speaking, we tend to say that we won't go *into* the house of pornography or sexual immorality, we'll just pass *by* it, we'll only go *near* its door. We want to test the waters and get as close as we can to the boundary line without crossing it. We just want to look over the fence to see what's on the other side, while telling ourselves that we won't actually go over. What ends up happening more often than not is we go inside the house, we jump the fence, we cross the line into the territory of sin. This is why Solomon admonishes us to not even go near the door of the house of these sins. Make no provision for the flesh.

If you recall from earlier in this chapter, we see a common thread between Samson and David and their eyes. David and Samson were not alone. It's common among sinful humans to look at things that are off-limits. Therefore, we must be ever so valiant in guarding our eyes. As the old children's church song says, "Oh, be careful little eyes what you see."

A Dead-End Road

The road that leads to sexual immorality is the same road that leads to destruction. So then, are you looking for ways to destroy your life? If so, then it's quite simple: just give yourself over to the lusts of the eyes and flesh, and stroll down the path that leads to sexual immorality. But just remember two things: first, that "her house leads down to death, and her paths to the dead; none who go to her return, nor do they regain the paths of life" (Prov 2:18-19); second, when the destruction and misery and regret come, don't say you weren't warned.

6

THE LIFE-SAVING ALTERNATIVE: PURITY

Because a significant portion of the previous chapter provided helpful solutions in battling lust, pornography, and sexual immorality, there's no need to be redundant here. Nevertheless, a few more helpful points can be made. How do we avoid and protect ourselves from the various forms of sexual immorality? Let's examine two ways in particular.

Heed Wisdom

In each of the major passages where Solomon warns his son of the immoral woman (2:16-19; 5:1-20; 6:24-35; 7:1-26), the main thing he says will save a person from the vile sin of sexual immorality is listening to and heeding wisdom. For example, Solomon declares, "When wisdom enters your heart, … understanding will keep you, … to deliver you from the immoral woman" (2:10, 11, 16). Therefore, how can we steer ourselves away from sexual immorality? Seek wisdom, pay attention to wisdom, heed wisdom.

Fear the Lord

We don't need to go into a full explanation of what the fear of the Lord is since it was discussed in chapter one. Nevertheless, an important point should be made here. In Psalm 119:9, David asked and answered, "How can a young person stay on the path of purity? By living according to your word" (NIV). In other words, the way that we live and maintain a life of purity is by listening to and obeying God's Word. To do this requires the fear of the Lord. In case you forgot, the fear of the Lord is to believe that God will do what He has said in His Word, and to then put that belief into action by obeying what it says.

Helpful Tips and Steps to Take

You may have noticed that in the sections dealing with the heart, mind, and eyes, a theme I repeated over and over again was the need to *guard* these areas of our lives. If it can be said that this is one of the greatest necessities in the Christian life, then one of the most important questions that can be asked on this topic is, How do we do this? In other words, *how* do we guard our hearts, minds, and eyes? It isn't enough to know *that* we need to do something, though this is important. We must also be equipped with skill knowledge, i.e., we need to know *how-to* do it.[38] Therefore, the remainder of this chapter will provide a few helpful tips and steps to take in answer to the question of *how to* guard ourselves.

1. *Trash the Trash*

Maybe it goes without saying how important this first tip is. It may seem like the most obvious step to take, but it needs to be mentioned nonetheless. Get rid of the garbage, the things that are

---

[38] In epistemology, which is one of the primary areas of philosophy, there are three types of knowledge. The first is *propositional* knowledge, which is know *that* something is true. In the context above, an example of propositional knowledge is knowing *that* we need to guard our hearts, minds, and eyes. The second type of knowledge is called *skill* knowledge. This is knowing *how to* do something, e.g., knowing *how* to guard ourselves. We need both types of knowledge in order to effectively obey the Lord in guarding ourselves from sin.

stumbling blocks for you and that cause you to fall into temptation. Paul exhorts us, "Therefore, having these promises, beloved, let us cleanse ourselves from all filthiness of the flesh and spirit, perfecting holiness in the fear of God" (2 Cor 7:1). James also commands, "Therefore lay aside all filthiness and overflow of wickedness, and receive with meekness the implanted word, which is able to save your souls" (Jas 1:21).

Whether you're dealing with lust, fornication, adultery, or pornography, you know that there are certain things—e.g., unmonitored internet access on a phone or computer, certain apps, specific people, and so on—that serve as doorways to these sins. When you're around those things, you end up stumbling into sin more often than not. Therefore, do as Paul and James say and lay aside—or get rid of—*all* of the filthiness and sinful pollution that you know is an avenue for you to sin. Don't be content with getting rid of some of it but leaving other avenues open. If you give the flesh an inch, it'll take a mile.

And it isn't just the inherently sinful things that we need to lay aside. Some things that aren't sinful in and of themselves can still be a stumbling block for some of us. Ponder the words of Hebrews 12:1, "Therefore we also, since we are surrounded by so great a cloud of witnesses, let us lay aside every weight, and the sin which so easily ensnares *us,* and let us run with endurance the race that is set before us." Notice the distinction the author makes between *weight* and *sin.* In other words, *sin* is very obviously sin, but *weights* don't have to be inherently sinful things. They could consist of something that is neither good nor bad but, for you personally, it weighs you down and causes you to sin. For example, Instagram (or whatever social media platform you use) isn't sinful in and of itself. It's a-moral. It can be used for evil and it can be used for good. However, if you struggle with lust and/or pornography, Instagram might be a weight—or a stumbling block—for you because when you go on the app, you end up seeing, gazing, watching, and then fantasizing about various images you come across while using the app—even though Instagram isn't inherently evil.

There may be certain things that aren't inherently evil but are stumbling blocks for you personally at various periods in your life.[39] What should you do about those things? If they're causing you to sin, then I think you *know* what you need to do with them. Romans 13:14 says, "But put on the Lord Jesus Christ, and make no provision for the flesh, to *fulfill its* lusts." If those things are making provision for your flesh, rather than the Holy Spirit, to influence you and to rule over you, then they have got to go. You may be thinking, "But I love these things so much and my life would be so boring without them." Consider this: is it really worth it to keep that thing—whatever it may be—around if it's causing you to sin and, in turn, doing damage to your relationship with God?[40]

---

[39] It should be noted that though some a-moral "weights" may be stumbling blocks for you *now*, that doesn't necessarily mean they will *always* be so. For example, you may not be able to handle having an Instagram account right *now* in life, but it may not be an issue later in life. You must exercise great caution and discernment here. Don't think that because you're strong one day, you'll be strong every day. Do as John Calvin said and *know yourself*. Know your limits, know what you can and can't handle, and guard against self-deception, i.e., deceiving yourself into thinking that you can handle something even though deep down you know you can't.

[40] An important point should be made here. Just because something a-moral may be a stumbling block for *you* and may cause *you* to sin, that doesn't mean it is a temptation and stumbling block for *everyone*. Therefore, be careful of imposing your own convictions upon other people simply because *you* struggle with certain things that aren't inherently sinful. For example, let's say that you have the personal conviction that you should not have an Instagram account, at least not for this season of your life, because when you open the app, you end up stumbling into the sin of lust. If that is your conviction then, by all means, get rid of Instagram. However, be careful not to impose your conviction on others by telling them that it is sinful for *them* to have an Instagram account. Just because you stumble when using the app, that doesn't mean that everyone else stumbles when using it as well. As another example, let's say you live

2. Accountability

God created humans for community. We need each other. God never intended for us to go through the Christian life in the lone-ranger-style. He created us as a body to work together, to build each other up, to strengthen each other. Solomon says, "*As* iron sharpens iron, so a man sharpens the countenance of his friend" (Prov 27:17). Therefore, a major step toward walking in victorious purity is to seek accountability from people.

Obviously, you need to be careful about who you choose for accountability partners. You don't want to reveal your struggles to a gossip who will go around sharing your deepest secrets with everyone. Also, avoid choosing someone of the opposite sex to keep you accountable in matters of sexual impurity. In addition to these tips, be careful not to choose *yes-men* for accountability partners. Choose people who love you enough to speak truth to you, even if it hurts. In Proverbs 27:5-6, Solomon wisely says, "Open rebuke *is* better than love carefully concealed. Faithful *are* the wounds of a friend, but the kisses of an enemy *are* deceitful." Your best friend is oftentimes the one who will tell you the most truth. One final point: as much as is possible, choose accountability partners who will *actually* hold you accountable. Avoid people who say they'll hold you accountable but then never check up on you.

---

near the beach and in the summertime, you like to go with your friends but you struggle with lust. If you have the personal conviction that you shouldn't be near the beach for a season of your life because you can't control your eyes while being there, then it's okay not to go. However, it is wrong to impose that same conviction on your friends and tell them it's sinful for *them* to go to the beach because there are many opportunities for temptation there and they're just bound to fall. If it is your personal conviction, then follow that conviction and yield to the Holy Spirit, but don't impose your conviction on your friends. It would be a different case if the beach was a specifically sinful place such as a strip club, but it is not. The beach is not evil.

3. Avoid Stupid Situations

Don't place yourself in a situation where you'll be tempted. If you tend to sin sexually or by viewing pornography when you're alone, then try your best to avoid being home by yourself. This may not always be possible but when it is and when you're feeling tempted, it's probably a good idea to get out of the house and go somewhere public. I understand that this may not always work, so here are some other tips when you're feeling tempted: pray and open up the Word and renew your mind with God's truth. Also, call up your accountability partner and ask for prayer.

If you have been tempted and have possibly even fallen into sexual immorality with a person when you're left alone with them, then avoid situations where you're alone with that person. Whenever hanging out with that person, make sure other people are hanging out with the two of you or that you're in public.

4. Don't Eat Your Barf

In Proverbs 26:11, Solomon says, "As a dog returns to his own vomit, so a fool repeats his folly." Whatever form of sexual immorality you may struggle with, once you take the first step of getting rid of it, don't return to the vomit. Just as it's disgusting that a dog eats his own barf, and just as it's a shame when a fool goes back to his foolishness, so also it is foolishness and a shame when we go back to our sin to which we were once enslaved. A striking question for you to ponder when you're thinking of going back to old sins: "So what benefit did you then reap from those things that you are now ashamed of? For the end of those things is death" (Rom 6:21 NET).

As I said earlier in this chapter, one of the temptations of sin is that it only ever tells you how much fun it'll be and how enjoyable it was last time. It never tells you of the pain, shame, regret, and consequences you experienced last time. When you're victorious, the temptation will eventually come back and, when it does, remember the slavery into which it brought you; remember the regret, the consequences, the guilt. And when you remember it, do as Paul commands, "Flee sexual immorality" (1 Cor 6:18a).

A Final Thought

Maybe you're feeling a bit overwhelmed or even discouraged here, wondering how in the world you'll be able to overcome temptation and to walk in holiness before the Lord, especially when looking back on all the previous times you've fallen so short and missed the mark. Dear reader, be encouraged with a wonderful promise from God's Word: "No temptation has overtaken you except such as is common to man; but God is faithful, who will not allow you to be tempted beyond what you are able, but with the temptation will also make the way of escape, that you may be able to bear it" (1 Cor 10:13). This verse has oft been misquoted by many Christians. They say something like, "It says in the Bible that God will never give you more than you can handle." That is not at all what Paul says here. In fact, there are many times in life when God gives us more than we can handle on our own so that we learn to trust in Him and not in our own strength. What Paul is saying is that God won't let the Christian be tempted beyond what they're able to endure, and that is an encouraging thought. And remember, God is faithful. He will always, with every temptation you face, provide an escape route. Therefore, when being tempted, look for the escape route and take it. And always remember that He is with you and He will never leave you nor forsake you. Be strong not in your own power but in the strength of Christ. Be totally dependent on the Holy Spirit for help, for it is only by doing this that you'll experience true victory over sin.

One final thought. Maybe you have committed the physical sin of sexual immorality in your past. After reading the previous chapter

and all the passages from Proverbs dealing with the terrible consequences of sexual immorality, maybe you're feeling pretty hopeless.
If this describes your present state, there is hope. Jesus died for all
sin, including sexual immorality, and His blood is more than able to
wash away the stains of this sin. This doesn't mean we should treat
this sin carelessly and it also doesn't mean that just because there is
forgiveness, there aren't consequences to sin. But there is a beautiful promise in Proverbs 28:13, wherein Solomon says, "He who
covers his sins will not prosper, but whoever confesses and forsakes them will have mercy." The first part of the verse should
serve as a warning, the second part as hope. If you repent of your
sin, there is forgiveness, mercy, and healing from God. If you have
fallen into sexual immorality or have sinned with your eyes by lust-
ing and viewing pornography, don't waste more time wallowing in
the guilt and shame. Rather, be quick to humble yourself,
acknowledge and confess your sin, repent, recognize the grace of
God and His forgiveness of your sin, and press on in the fight. Finally, remember Paul's words in Romans 8:34-35, 37-39:

> Who *is* he who condemns? It is Christ who died, and fur-
> thermore is also risen, who is even at the right hand of
> God, who also makes intercession for us. Who shall sepa-
> rate us from the love of Christ? Shall tribulation, or dis-
> tress, or persecution, or famine, or nakedness, or peril, or
> sword? Yet in all these things we are more than conquer-
> ors through Him who loved us. For I am persuaded that
> neither death nor life, nor angels nor principalities nor
> powers, nor things present nor things to come, nor height
> nor depth, nor any other created thing, shall be able to
> separate us from the love of God which is in Christ Jesus
> our Lord.

7

CROOKEDNESS KILLS

A worthless person, a wicked man, walks with a perverse mouth;
He winks with his eyes, he shuffles his feet, he points with his fingers;
Perversity is in his heart, he devises evil continually, he sows discord.
Therefore his calamity shall come suddenly;
Suddenly he shall be broken without remedy.

Proverbs 6:12-15

The way of the LORD is strength for the upright,
But destruction will come to the workers of iniquity.

Proverbs 10:29

The integrity of the upright will guide them,
But the perversity of the unfaithful will destroy them.

Proverbs 11:3

It is a joy for the just to do justice,
But destruction will come to the workers of iniquity.

Proverbs 21:15

All of the above passages share one common theme, namely, that destruction will come to the perverse person. *Perversity* is the key word of this chapter. It's a word that isn't as commonly used today as it was in the past. Most people probably couldn't even define it if they were asked.

The Hebrew words used for *perverse* in Proverbs 6:12, 14, and 11:3 denote *crookedness* or *crooked dealing, distortion, deceit,* and *fraud*. According to the dictionary, *perverse* has several meanings:

- directed away from what is right or good;
- perverted;
- obstinately persisting in an error or fault;
- wrongly self-willed or stubborn;
- marked by a disposition to oppose and contradict.

Remember that one purpose of this book is to show you six definite ways to destroy your life. Therefore, if this is your personal aim, then simply live a perverse life as defined above and you're guaranteed to succeed in destroying your life. Though people often think of perversity only in the extreme sense of the word, don't be fooled into thinking that this chapter doesn't apply to you if you don't commit acts of what most people think are extremely perverse. There are degrees of perversity as there are degrees of other sins, but even those sins we consider to be "smaller scale" are still perversions of how God created us to live.

The 4 Characteristics of the Perverse Person

In Proverbs 2:10-15, Solomon says that qualities such as wisdom, knowledge, discretion, and understanding will protect and "deliver you from the way of evil, from the man who speaks perverse things, from those who leave the paths of uprightness to walk in the ways of darkness; who rejoice in doing evil, and delight in the perversity of the wicked; whose ways are crooked, and who are devious in their paths." Let's examine four of the most defining characteristics of a perverse person.

Characteristic #1: Gravitation Toward Evil

The perverse person is constantly drawn toward the way of unrighteousness and evil. Recall a couple of the previous definitions of perverse: *directed away from what is right or good; obstinately persisting in an error or fault.* A perverse person is constantly gravitating away from what is right and good and, as a result, choosing evil paths. This corresponds exactly with how Solomon describes perverse people in Proverbs 2:13, that they "leave the paths of uprightness to walk in the ways of darkness." It's important to note that leaving the right way and traversing the path of evil is an intentional decision on the part of perverse people.

There really are only two paths in life: the path of *righteousness*—or uprightness—and the path of *unrighteousness*—or evil. Jesus Himself made this point in the Sermon on the Mount when He declared, "Enter by the narrow gate; for wide is the gate and broad is the way that leads to destruction, and there are many who go in by it. Because narrow is the gate and difficult is the way which leads to life, and there are few who find it" (Matt 7:13-14). Following Christ leads to life, whereas following the ways of the world leads to destruction. Therefore, when a person turns off the path of righteousness, the obvious result is that he'll turn onto the path of evil. And not only this, but the perverse person is also *attracted* to evil. A perverse person is drawn toward evil like a moth is drawn to a light. And it doesn't stop at mere attraction. The attraction leads to action, which leads us to the second characteristic of the perverse person.

Characteristic #2: Schemer

People who are *drawn to* evil will be *influenced by* evil and then it's only a matter of time until they start *doing* evil. Such is the case of the perverse person. He/she isn't satisfied with merely being attracted or drawn to evil. Recall from Proverbs 2:14 that the perverse person rejoices and delights in two things: (1) doing evil, and (2) watching other people do evil. Proverbs 10:23 says, "To do evil is like sport to a fool." Ponder this question as a point of application: what brings you joy and happiness in life? For the perverse fool, doing evil is what brings him/her the greatest pleasure in life.

A defining characteristic of perverse people is that they don't just commit evil absent-mindedly without giving it any thought; rather, they *plan* or *scheme* to do evil things. They're "are devious in their paths" (Prov 2:15) and they "devise evil continually" (Prov 6:14). It's one thing to commit an act of evil in the spur of the moment without giving it any thought. It's quite another thing—and much worse, I might add—to sit around planning and plotting evil before carrying it out. In legal terms, this is known as premeditated evil.

Perverse people are in a constant habit of planning evil schemes, much like the Devil. They plan out their evil actions, they carefully ponder how to be most effective in their evil plots, they meditate on how to cover up their actions and get away with their crimes. The perverse heart is really a reflection of the heart of Satan, and it is totally contrary to the heart of God. It's little wonder, then, why such actions produce such destructive consequences. In fact, Proverbs 10:29 declares, "The way of the LORD is like a stronghold for the upright, but it is destruction to evildoers." (NET) Why is the way of God destruction to evildoers? The reason is simply because evildoers don't walk in the way of God but in the ways of evil. Connect the dots: if the way of evil is the exact opposite of God's way and if God's way is like a stronghold—or a secure, safe fortress—then, logically, the way of evil is like an insecure, broken down, defeated place.

Characteristic #3: Crookedness

One of the definitions of *perverse* at the beginning of this chapter is *perverted*. In today's society the term *pervert* is used almost always in only one way, namely, with reference to some kind of sexual perversion. Though this is an accurate use of the term, the word actually has a much broader meaning. To *pervert* something means to corrupt, distort, or alter something from its original course, meaning, or state and from what was originally intended. This is a very apt description of the perverse person. God created people to live righteously and to reflect His character well. Therefore, the actions and lifestyle of a perverse person are a distortion and corruption of the way God originally intended for people to live. Solomon summarizes this concept in Ecclesiastes 7:29 when he says, "Truly, this only I have found: that God made man upright, but they have sought out many schemes." This is the exact idea behind perversity and perversion. They're the stark contrast of the upright lifestyle God originally intended for mankind to live.

Recall Proverbs 11:3, wherein Solomon states, "The integrity of the upright will guide them, but the perversity of the unfaithful will destroy them." The main contrast is between the upright man and the perverse man. The key words are *integrity*, *upright*, *perversity*, and *unfaithful*.

The life of the upright man is defined by integrity. *Integrity* is the characteristic of being honest and doing the right thing no matter who is or isn't around. It means to be undivided and wholly steadfast in your determination to do righteousness and be blameless. Regarding *uprightness*, consider the anatomical aspect behind the word. The idea of *upright* is to stand straight up, not crookedly or hunched over. The emphasis is on perfect straightness. It's the same concept when using the word to discuss issues of morality. Uprightness means to walk and live in a morally straight, righteous, good way and to be innocent of dealing crookedly, dishonestly, or unjustly.

To be perverse, on the other hand, is to live in the exact opposite manner of the upright person. In fact, several other translations of Proverbs 11:3 use the word *crookedness* instead of *perversity*.[41] The opposite of crooked is straight. An object that is upright—or straight—is always consistently going the same direction, whereas with crookedness, it can always be shifting and changing direction. You never know which way the object will go.

Think of Jack Sparrow's compass in the movie, *The Pirates of the Caribbean*. A good-working compass always reliably points straight in the same direction—north. Jack's compass, however, was crooked, so to speak. There were times here and there when it pointed north, but it also, almost constantly, pointed in wrong directions as well. It steered Jack and his companions off course from the right way. Therefore, it was crooked and it couldn't be relied on to be upright, i.e., to point in the correct direction. The same is true of people with regard to their *moral* compass.

A straight shooter—i.e., upright person—can always be counted on to do what's right and just and good. Upright people are reliable to consistently go in one direction, that of righteousness. In contrast, people who are crooked in their ways are shifty and cannot be counted on to be honest, upright, and to have integrity. You never know which way they'll go, morally speaking. They may, at times, do the right thing, but there's no guarantee. This is why they're unreliable and are referred to as being *crooked*.

Many times throughout the Bible, the term *crooked* is used to describe wicked people who wander from the paths of truth, righteousness, justice, and uprightness. Consider the following examples:

---

[41] See the NASB, NET, and the ESV.

- "They have corrupted themselves; they are not His children, because of their blemish: a perverse and crooked generation." (Deut 32:5)
- "The way of a guilty man is crooked, but as for the pure, his conduct is upright." (Prov 21:8 NASB)
- "Better is the poor who walks in his integrity than he who is crooked though he be rich." (Prov 28:6 NASB)
- "He who walks blamelessly will be delivered, but he who is crooked will fall all at once." (Prov 28:18 NASB)
- "Those of crooked heart are an abomination to the LORD, but those of blameless ways are his delight." (Prov 11:20 ESV)
- "The way of peace they have not known, and there is no justice in their ways; they have made themselves crooked paths; whoever takes that way shall not know peace." (Isa 59:8)
- "…that you may become blameless and harmless, children of God without fault in the midst of a crooked and perverse generation, among whom you shine as lights in the world." (Phil 2:15)

Perverse people are crooked not only in their personal lives but also in their dealings with other people. They're dishonest and unjust. They do shady business. Recall the meanings of the Hebrew words used in Proverbs for perverse: *crooked dealing, deceit,* and *fraud.*

Are there consequences for living crookedly? You better believe there are. David foretells, "As for such as turn aside to their crooked ways, the LORD shall lead them away with the workers of iniquity" (Ps 125:5). When it says that God will lead them away, the connotation is that they're being led away to judgment and destruction.

Characteristic #4: Unteachable

The perverse person is also unteachable. Recall the following definitions of perverse: *obstinately persisting in an error or fault; wrongly self-willed or stubborn; marked by a disposition to oppose and contradict.*

Perverse people are hard-headed, arrogant, stubborn, unteachable fools. They will obstinately continue doing, saying, and/or believing something that is wrong or false even after being shown that they're wrong. Why do they do this? It's because they are unteachable. They've already made up their mind to oppose you, no matter how wise your counsel may be. Nothing can change their mind. They have a disposition to go against all wise counsel. In fact, Solomon wisely states, "He who separates himself seeks his own desire, he quarrels against all sound wisdom" (Prov 18:1 NASB). Perverse people choose to go against the flow and rebel simply for the sake of rebelling. Oftentimes the perverse person doesn't care about truth and finding out the facts and then conforming his/her life and views to the truth. Instead, he/she just wants to argue and to be contrary.

Paying the High Price

Every action has consequences. It's clearly stated throughout Scripture that people will one day be judged by God for their actions on earth. Your actions come at a cost, even if you don't experience the consequences immediately. Oftentimes when people do evil and don't experience immediate negative repercussions, they think that they got away with it, and so they continue down a path of making sinful decisions. But there's a price to pay for your actions, and perversity comes at a high price. Living perversely may be fun, enjoyable, even exhilarating in the moment, but it all comes with a severe cost. Try to find what each of the following verses have in common:

- "The way of the LORD is…destruction to evildoers." (Prov 10:29 NET)
- "The perversity of the unfaithful will destroy them." (Prov 11:3)
- "Destruction will come to the workers of iniquity." (Prov 21:15)
- "Therefore his calamity shall come suddenly; suddenly he shall be broken without remedy." (Prov 6:15; the NIV renders this verse, "Therefore disaster will overtake him in an instant; he will suddenly be destroyed—without remedy.")

The common theme in all these verses is the promise that destruction comes to the evil, perverse person. And if God makes a promise, you can bet your life that He'll fulfill it. Therefore, if you want to destroy yourself, then simply live a lifestyle that is marked by perversity.

Perverse people will be destroyed because they choose to live lives fully submerged in wickedness. They constantly indulge in evil practices. They love the way of evil. Remember that the way of evil is the exact opposite of God's way, which is the way of light and truth. Therefore, the way of evil and perversity is the way of darkness and lies. Imagine trying to run down an unfamiliar path is total darkness. To walk on the path of evil is to walk in spiritual darkness and, as a result, to be blind. Mankind's greatest need is to get to God and walk in His light. Walking down the path of evil is to blindly walk further and further away from God and His light and truth. And that path leads only to destruction. Furthermore, Solomon tells us that "the perverse person is an abomination to the LORD" (Prov 3:32). To live perversely, then, is to make yourself abhorrent to God and to become His enemy, and there is only one way that that lifestyle ends.

8

THE LIFE-SAVING ALTERNATIVE: UPRIGHTNESS

The alternative to destroying your life through perverse and evil living is to shun perversity and to walk uprightly. Remember that living wisely leads to life, as we discussed in chapter one. The key, then, to choosing life over destruction is to walk in wisdom and be wise. But what does it mean to walk in wisdom? What does that look like on a practical level?

Let's begin by asking, where does wisdom begin? Solomon says, "The fear of the LORD is the beginning of wisdom" (Prov 9:10). Thus, one of the most fundamental components of godly wisdom is the fear—or high reverence—of the Lord. And what does the fear of the Lord look like, practically speaking? In Proverbs 8:13, personified wisdom declares, "The fear of the LORD is to hate evil." Do you see the connection? The way you can you save yourself from a fate of destruction due to perverse and evil living is to fear God, which is to hate evil.

Notice something very important about Proverbs 8:13. *Refraining from doing* evil is only part of what it means to fear God. The biblical fear of the Lord involves *hating* evil as well. There's an important distinction between the two. You can love evil but choose not to do it, but this isn't the idea behind a true fear of God. A person who fears and follows God is a person who strives to be like God in His character, in His thoughts, and in His attitude. This is what we mean when we say a person is *god-ly*. Therefore, a true God-fearer strives to daily have his/her heart and mind transformed so that he/she views the world through God's perspective.

What is God's perspective—or view or attitude—on evil? He hates it. Therefore, to fear God means not only to *not do* evil, but to truly *hate* evil as well. Do you have a godly hatred of evil? Think of some of the sins that you find yourself going back to frequently, and ask, *Do I truly hate these evil sins?* Do you want to save yourself from destruction? If *yes*, then be a wise person, and be a wise person by fearing God, and fear God by hating evil.

Now, the question arises, how do I hate evil? Good question, I'm glad you asked. Answering this question is somewhat complicated because it has to do with changing our attitude, and changing our attitude usually isn't as quick and easy as, say, turning on or off a light switch. Rather, it usually takes time, a lot of prayer, and practice. In short, it can be a difficult task.

To give a personal example, my wife, Courtney, and I used to live in a small condo with bad insulation and an extremely small kitchen (Courtney loves cooking, baking, and everything in the kitchen, so having such a small kitchen space drives her crazy). We went out of state to visit a family who has a two-story house with five bedrooms, three bathrooms, a large kitchen, two living rooms, and more. While we were standing in their kitchen one day, Courtney jokingly (but somewhat seriously) said to me, "I'm having a hard time not coveting having a house like this." I somewhat jokingly (but somewhat seriously) responded, "Then just don't covet." About two seconds later I realized how stupid and unhelpful my advice was. Courtney had an *attitude* of covetousness. Therefore, to truly help Courtney change her attitude from being covetous to being content required a lot more than simply telling her not to covet.

Most people, upon hearing my horrible four-worded advice, would not have an instant attitude change. Why not? The reason is because our attitudes flow from our heart and mind, and it tends to take a lot of slow-going, detailed work to transform those two areas of our lives. Therefore, the question of how to hate evil is more complex than it might seem. It requires careful attention and detailed thought in order to come up with helpful solutions. Learning to hate evil is just that, a learning process.

All growth takes time, and is never instantaneous. It takes a lot of learning and practice and help from the Holy Spirit to grow in our hatred of evil. In all reality, it's a lifelong pursuit and process of being transformed by Christ. But there are attitudes, habits, and practices that we can implement and incorporate into our lives *now* that will help speed up our growing process in learning to hate evil more *in the future.*

Let's finish this chapter by examining three steps we can take toward growth in our hatred of evil. However, keep in mind that such growth can happen only through our hearts and minds being yielded to and transformed by the Holy Spirit.

Step One: Vision

One of the most foundational changes that needs to happen in order for us to hate evil more is that we need to see evil the way God sees evil. Because of our sinful nature, we naturally don't see evil the way God sees it—at least, we don't see *all* evil the way He sees it.[42] Solomon rightly says, "There is a way that seems right to a man, but its end is the way of death" (Prov 14:12; 16:25). What Solomon is saying is that people naturally think that their sinful ways, which lead to death, are actually good, right, and morally acceptable. This is due to the fact that they don't see evil the way

---

[42] For example, because we're created in God's image and have a conscience, we do intuitively know that certain evil acts are, in fact, evil (e.g., murder, torturing children for fun, etc.).

God sees it. They have a sinful, fleshly worldview. Thus, people have a desperate need to look at evil through a different lens, namely, God's lens. Looking through God's lens is to see evil the way it is in truth.

So then, how can we get to the point where we view evil the way God views it? How can we look through God's lens? These are both application questions, and they can be answered in our next two steps.

Step Two: Know God More

Because of our sinful nature, we naturally love evil and spiritual darkness rather than good and light. Jesus said, "And this is the condemnation, that the light has come into the world, and men loved darkness rather than light, because their deeds were evil. For everyone practicing evil hates the light and does not come to the light, lest his deeds should be exposed" (John 3:19-20). Thus, we have a desperate need for transformation. The first major transformation is the salvation-transformation, where we pass from spiritual death and darkness into spiritual life and light by trusting in Christ to save us from our sin. The next major transformation is a daily, rest-of-your-life kind of sanctification-transformation process where we grow in our relationship with God as we forsake our old "works of darkness" (Rom 13:12; Eph 5:11) and choose to "Walk as children of light" (Eph 5:8).

The more you get to know God, the more your attitude will change and become like God's attitude, your views will conform to His views, and your will shall conform to His will. The more you get to know God and conform your life to be more and more like Him, the more naturally you will love what God loves and hate what He hates. This is one of the most fundamental ways to grow in your hatred of evil. You become like the company you keep. If you spend a lot of time with God, you will start thinking the way God thinks on various issues.

Now, the question arises, how do we get to know God more? And how can we look at evil through God's lens? Both questions have the same answer: the Bible. If the Bible is God's revelation of Himself to us, then one of the greatest ways to get to know Him more is by studying this amazing love letter He has given to us. Similarly, we can learn to view evil through God's lens by studying the Bible since, in it, God repeatedly reveals His standards regarding various thoughts, beliefs, and actions that are either good or evil. The Bible is rightly called God's Word, and in this Book God reveals His view—the right view—on various beliefs and actions that are evil. Therefore, if you want to look through God's lens to see how He defines evil, study His Word.

Another way we can know God better is through intentional prayer and meditation—not the Buddhist-type meditation. Prayer is communication with God and meditation—in the biblical sense— is pondering or thinking deeply about God and the things of God. It is to give all of your attention and thought to godliness and spiritual growth.

Prayer consists not only of making requests of God, though this unfortunately seems to be what fills the majority of our prayer time. Though prayer partially consists of asking God for things, there is much more to it than that. Prayer is speaking to God, thanking God, recognizing how great and good and awesome God is, interceding to God, and—the one we like least—waiting on God. Have you ever stopped in your prayers to spend just 10 minutes not asking God for anything but simply doing nothing but waiting on Him? Do it. And don't just try it once, but make it a regular practice. The more time you spend with God in His presence, the more your life will be conformed to love what He loves and to hate what He hates. Furthermore, the more time you spend with God in His presence, the more you will see just how evil your sins are as you view them against the backdrop of the holiness of

God.

Step Three: Filters

Changing our attitude usually takes a lot of time and practice. A helpful practice to aid you is to filter your intake. In other words, pay attention to and be careful of what you allow into your life. By way of analogy, let's say you have a horrible diet. The majority of your food intake consists of junk food. Rarely do you consume healthy foods. You know you have a problem and you are motivated to fix it, but you're not sure how. You begin by recognizing that the foundation of your problem is that your *attitude* toward food is wrong. In fact, it's all backwards from what it's supposed to be. You love junk and you hate the good, healthy stuff. Therefore, to help change your attitude toward food, you start changing your intake of foods. You start rejecting junk and making yourself eat only the healthy stuff. It'll no doubt be painstakingly hard in the beginning, as the good stuff seems bland and you crave the junk, but over time you'll recognize a change in your attitude toward good and bad foods. You'll start to enjoy some of those healthier foods and your body will feel better and more energized as well. At the same time, you'll grow to have more of a distaste for a lot of the junk foods you used to eat.

To give you a personal example of this from my own life, I love sugar (I've been cursed with a major sweet tooth). A couple years ago I was motivated to start eating healthier by eating less sugar. I started by looking at the ingredients in the foods I ate. I looked at my peanut butter jar and was shocked to see how much sugar they add to their peanut butter (there's more sugar than there are peanuts!). I decided to go to Costco and buy a jar of organic peanut butter that had only two ingredients: peanuts and salt. Pretty bland, right? It looked like "normal" peanut butter, so I figured it would taste the same. It tasted terrible. I hated it and left it on my shelf for about a year. I finally decided to try it again and forced myself to eat it. I refused to buy the brand I liked because I knew that if it was in the house, I'd go back to my old habits of sugar butter—I mean, less healthy peanut butter. After a couple of months, I was at someone's house and had a bite of the more sugary peanut butter and, guess what. I hated it. It tasted gross to me. Why? Over time and lots of practice and discipline, my mind, body, and attitude adapted and shifted to enjoying the healthy peanut butter to the point where *I didn't even miss the old stuff.* And then, when I tried the junk after only having the healthy stuff, it was way too sweet for me and now, I refuse to eat the junk.

The same concept is true in our spiritual lives. A helpful way to change your attitude toward evil is to start by doing a thorough inventory of the content intake of your eyes, ears, and mind. In other words, what kind of content are you taking into your life when you watch movies or TV, listen to music, listen to your friends, and so on? What is your content intake on a daily or weekly basis? If you notice a lot of junk (i.e., stuff that is pulling you down in your pursuit of following Jesus) rather than a lot of stuff that is godly and edifying to your soul, then it's time to clean house.

My Challenge to You

Here is a challenge for you. For the next week or month, get rid of whatever content you take in that fits into the category of "evil" (and remember, evil is simply anything that dishonors God and is contrary to His way), and don't give yourself any opportunity to go back to it in a moment of weakness (you may need an accountability partner). Then, fill all that new, empty time with good, edifying things. Some examples might include going to church more often, looking for ways to serve others in your church, listening to more edifying music, studying your Bible more, getting outdoors and enjoying the beauty of God's creation, joining a Bible study and/or having some theological discussions with some friends, researching and learning more about the Church and Church history, and studying apologetics. At the end of your designated time that you choose to complete this challenge, take inventory again and answer the following questions:

- How did I do in getting rid of the junk and then filling my life with only good, edifying things?
- Has my attitude changed at all toward evil?
- As a result of changing my habits during this challenge, have I grown to love these good things more than I did before?
- Have I grown in my relationship with Jesus?
- Have I grown in my relationships with and love for people?
- Do other people notice a change in me? (This obviously requires you to ask people this question rather than to answer it yourself.)

A Final Thought

While examining Proverbs 6:14 in the previous chapter, we discovered that the perverse person has a crooked heart. King David prayed that God would give him a heart that was the exact opposite of this, and I encourage you to ask God to do the same for you. In Psalm 51:10, David prays, "Create in me a clean heart, O God, and renew a steadfast spirit within me." In Psalm 101:4, David says, "A perverse heart shall depart from me; I will not know wickedness." That's an incredible declaration! That is the life-saving alternative. Finally, in Psalm 57:7, David declares, "My heart is steadfast, O God, my heart is steadfast; I will sing and give praise." A heart that is steadfast in obeying God is a heart that is firmly planted, grounded, rooted in truth, integrity, and doing what is right, no matter what. May this be true of our hearts!

9

TERROR IN THE TONGUE

He who guards his mouth preserves his life,
But he who opens wide his lips shall have destruction.

Proverbs 13:3

The wise person accepts instructions,
But the one who speaks foolishness will come to ruin.

Proverbs 10:8 (NET)

… foolish speech leads to imminent destruction.

Proverbs 10:14b (NET)

A fool's mouth is his destruction,
And his lips are the snare of his soul.

Proverbs 18:7

For a lot of people, some of their greatest regrets in life are linked to their mouth and things they've said in the past that they wish they could take back. Maybe you can relate. Countless relationships have been destroyed, bridges have been burned, deep and lifelong wounds have been inflicted, insecurities have been formed, all because of someone's words.

The question might be raised, what's so evil about the human tongue? Well, nothing, in and of itself. The tongue was created by God and can be used for so much good, such as spreading of Gospel, comforting and encouraging people, blessing others, standing up for the oppressed, giving positive motivation, and so on. But the tongue can also be used for endless evil. The tongue itself is not evil. Rather, it is *how we use it* and what it produces that is oftentimes evil rather than good.

One of the most valuable pieces of instruction you can receive regarding your tongue comes from James 1:19, where we are told to be "slow to speak." Why should we be slow to speak? Many of the following pages are dedicated to answering this question, but here is just one reason. It is because, as Solomon says, "In the multitude of words sin is not lacking" (Prov 10:19). In other words, where there is a lot of talk, there is bound to be sinful things that are said. The more you speak, the higher the chances that you'll say something foolish. More on that shortly. Let's now explore in greater depth why we should heed James's command to be slow to speak.

Power Beyond Reckoning

There is much that Solomon has to say in Proverbs about our words (see Appendix C for a detailed list of Proverbs about the tongue). Proverbs 18:21 contains one of the most profound realities about the power and potential that lies right within your own mouth. Solomon declares, "Death and life *are* in the power of the tongue, and those who love it will eat its fruit." Wow! Who knew that this tiny member of your body, weighing only a couple of ounces, has such great power to either destroy or give life to other people! Every time you open your mouth to speak, you have the power to speak life or death to people. Every person has this scary amount of power to cause horrid ruin and devastating damage to others without ever even lifting a finger. For, the damage that is caused by the tongue is not physical pain, but it is a sword that pierces the heart and breaks the spirit of a person.

The old saying that *sticks and stones may break my bones but words will never hurt me* is so untrue. Whoever came up with this saying had probably been severely hurt by other people's words and, rather than dealing with the pain the right way, made up this saying as a defense mechanism. Oftentimes it is people's words that hurt us far more than the physical pain they could inflict on us by physical abuse and violence. It is almost unimaginable just how much potential your tongue has to bring such mass amounts of hurt and destruction to people's lives. What are your words most often imparting to the lives of others: death or life?

To give you an example from my own life, when I was a teenager, I started playing guitar and leading worship at my youth group. Most of my friends constantly made fun of me and said I had a terrible singing voice, and the truth is that it was pretty bad at the time. However, their words and constant jokes at my expense were funny to them but very painful to me. From the very first time I was made fun of for my singing voice, insecurities started taking root and developing within me and each time a joke was made about my singing, those roots dug deeper and deeper. A few years later during my senior year of high school, I was asked to be one of the main worship leaders for our last school chapel of the year. This was a big moment for the seniors, as they were saying farewell to the rest of the school. Needless to say, I was excited for the chapel and thrilled to lead worship. The day before the chapel, however, a couple friends who were also seniors and in charge of planning and coordinating the chapel event called me and asked if the worship teacher could be the main singer instead of me. I asked why, though I had a good idea what their reasons were, based on my being made fun of in the past. One of my friends replied, not jokingly but in all seriousness, "Well, because we want someone who can actually sing."

The pain I experienced from my friend's words is difficult to put into words. Not to sound dramatic, but it pierced right to my heart. My friends probably didn't even think that their words would hurt me so much since they were unaware of my past experiences and insecurities. But, man, it hurt. When our phone call ended, I cried. I was embarrassed. I was humiliated. My self-consciousness about my singing grew even worse. All of these negative things took root within me long before and for many years they grew more and more after each time someone's unkind words about my singing reached my ears. And to this day, rarely but every now and then I still feel a little bit insecure when I stand up and start to sing when I lead worship.

My point is that it was the *words*, not physical violence, of others that caused so much hurt and insecurity in my life. And I shudder in horror and shame when I think of the fact that *my* words have caused the same kind of damage and pain to so many people so many times and that, many of those times, I don't even realize that my words have had such a devastating impact.

Think about this: so many of people's insecurities (including yours and mine) are rooted in the unkind words spoken by others. People's self-consciousness about various things in their lives are usually sourced in something mean and unkind that was said by others. Many people are self-conscious and insecure about one or more of their bodily features, including their hair, eyes, body type, body weight, height, their teeth, nose, smile, and so on. Many people also have insecurities regarding how they dress, the level of their intelligence, how athletic they are (or aren't), and so on because of hurtful things that have been said to or about them. Maybe you can relate?

Words are incredibly powerful, and can be incredibly painful. Here's a challenge for you: the next time you want to make fun—

whether jokingly or seriously—of someone, try to remember that when you jokingly make fun of someone and hurt that person, *you* usually forget about what you said almost instantly while continuing to go about your day as if nothing happened, but it's a very different situation for the people whom you hurt with your words. *They* don't forget what you said because it cut deep and hurt them. *They* will remember it long after you've forgotten it, and those piercing words will possibly negatively affect them for years to come, and your words will cause the roots of insecurity to run deeper and deeper. You know what I'm talking about because you've experienced this same thing in your own life when you've been made fun of. So, think before you speak.

The All-Consuming Tongue

In his epistle, James has some pretty sobering things to say about the dangerous potential the tongue has for evil. He begins by saying, "For we all stumble in many things. If anyone does not stumble in word, he *is* a perfect man, able also to bridle the whole body" (v. 2). The point James is making, as we will see, is that it's incredibly difficult to control the tongue and that if a person can master having control over his/her own tongue, then he/she can basically learn to control every other part of the body.

James now goes on to give two analogies from nature: "Indeed, we put bits in horses' mouths that they may obey us, and we turn their whole body. Look also at ships: although they are so large and are driven by fierce winds, they are turned by a very small rudder wherever the pilot desires. Even so the tongue is a little member and boasts great things" (vv. 3-5a). A bit is a piece of metal that you place into a horse's mouth. The bit is connected to the bridle and reins and it is by means of these tools that you a steer a horse in your desired direction when riding it. When you pull the reins back or side to side, the metal bit painfully crams into the back of the horse's mouth, causing it to yield to the direction the reins are pulling. Though the bit is so small, it can turn a huge horse. Similarly, though ships can be so large and seemingly immovable, yet they are moved by a comparatively tiny rudder. The point James is making is that the tongue is similar to bits and rudders: though it is such a small member of the human body, it can have such a profound influence.

James provides yet another analogy for his readers: "How great a forest is set ablaze by such a small fire! And the tongue is a fire, a world of unrighteousness. The tongue is set among our members, staining the whole body, setting on fire the entire course of life, and set on fire by hell" (vv. 5b-6 ESV). Being a Californian and living in the wildfire state, I know exactly what James is talking about. In fact, as I'm writing this chapter in 2020, many fires are burning down half of California. One of these fires, which is only a few miles from my home, was accidentally started by a small firework spark during a gender-reveal party for a baby. It really doesn't take much in the dry heat to start a blazing fire. And just as a little spark can turn into a blaze that ruins so much, so also the human tongue is so small but can bring such devastating destruction if not kept in check.

Furthermore, James tells us, "For every kind of beast and bird, of reptile and creature of the sea, is tamed and has been tamed by mankind. But no man can tame the tongue. *It is* an unruly evil, full of deadly poison. With it we bless our God and Father, and with it we curse men, who have been made in the similitude of God. Out of the same mouth proceed blessing and cursing. My brethren, these things ought not to be so" (vv. 7-10). How profound these words are indeed! Human beings have extraordinarily been able to tame all sorts of massive and dangerous animals. And yet, I don't know if such an amazing accomplishment should be viewed as impressive or embarrassing for the sole reason that for all the taming we can do of ferocious animals, we can't even control our own tiny tongues.

Our frequent hypocrisy is laid bare as James says that with the very mouth that we use to praise, worship, and bless God, we also curse and tear apart and belittle people who are created in God's image. Think about that! The apostle John writes, "If someone says, 'I love God,' and hates his brother, he is a liar; for he who does not love his brother whom he has seen, how can he love God whom he has not seen?" (1 John 4:20) Both John and James are getting at the same thing. If we bless God with our tongue and claim to love Him, the proof often will be in how we treat and speak to our fellow human beings. It is utter hypocrisy to honor God with our mouth and then turn around and speak in a sinful manner to or about other people.

When I was in Bible college, I remember hearing a story about one of the professors, Mark Schwartz. He was strolling through the campus one day when he overheard two students sitting at a table gossiping and talking badly about someone. Professor Schwartz walked up behind them, leaned down, asked in his deep, manly voice, "Do you bless God with that same mouth?" and then epically continued his stroll. Needless to say, I think the students got the point.

James finishes his discussion on the tongue with giving a few last analogies. "Does a spring send forth fresh *water* and bitter from the same opening? Can a fig tree, my brethren, bear olives, or a grapevine bear figs? Thus no spring yields both salt water and fresh" (vv. 11-12). The obvious answer to each of these questions is *no*. And the obvious point James is making is that just as a spring doesn't produce both fresh and bitter water, and just as a fig tree doesn't bear olives nor a grapevine bear figs, so also our tongues should not produce—or, speak—both righteousness and unrighteousness. If we claim to be followers of Christ, then we must be consistent in reflecting His character in how we speak.

So, I ask you, what frequently comes out of your mouth? Are you hypocritically blessing God with your mouth and then turning around and speaking wrongfully to or about people? Is your tongue out of control? To answer these questions effectively, you need to do some serious, in-depth self-examination. Also, ask these questions to the people who know you the best and find out what they say about you.

Death and life truly are in the power of your tiny tongue. James helps us see how often our tongues are used for evil to bring death to others. Just as there is incredible power in fire to consume and destroy an entire forest, so your tongue has immense power to bring ruin and death to others. No wonder James instructs us to be quick to hear and slow to speak (1:19).

Potential for Evil

Let's now examine just a few of the many ways in which we can use our tongues for evil and, in so doing, destroy not only our own lives but also the lives of others. As you read, do some thorough self-examination and ask the Lord to show you ways in which you've been guilty of using your tongue for evil.

Tearing Down

One of the most common ways people tend to use their tongue for evil is by tearing others down with unkind words. There are all kinds of ways we can do this. Sometimes friends will tear each other down jokingly, just messing around with each other and not meaning to hurt each other. Other times people will tear others down as a way to puff themselves up higher. They'll criticize others and minimize their efforts and accomplishments, while boasting about their own successes and exaggerating the greatness of their own accomplishments. Still other times people will be just plain nasty and rude, using their words to cut people down for seemingly no reason at all. In Proverbs 11:9, we read, "The hypocrite with *his* mouth destroys his neighbor." Is this true of you? Are you guilty of using your tongue to tear people down in any of the ways listed above? Who do you tend to tear down? And why? Dig deep and seriously think about these questions. Do the words you speak to others generally tend to build them up or tear them down?

Other times, we seek revenge against people for something unkind they did or said to us. We want to get them back 10 times worse, so we think of the ultimate insult to throw at them, whether it be commenting negatively on their appearance, bringing up an embarrassing mistake or a dark secret from their past to humiliate them, ridiculing a specific aspect of their character, lifestyle, or personality, and the list can go on and on. Two times Solomon says that "violence covers the mouth of the wicked" (Prov 10:6, 11). When we're angry and seeking revenge, we tend to use our words as a weapon to inflict painful wounds on the one with whom we're angry. In the heat of the moment, we can lose control of our mouth and say many terrible things that we regret later, and those wounds we inflict will often leave lasting scars.

Solomon has a lot to say about anger, self-control, and our words. In Proverbs 14:17, he says, "A quick-tempered *man* acts foolishly." Oftentimes, the way in which quick-tempered people act foolishly is through their words. Proverbs 15:18 (NASB) also says, "A hot-tempered man stirs up strife, but the slow to anger calms a dispute." The *New Living Translation* reads, "A hot-tempered person starts fights; a cool-tempered person stops them." Consider this: I think it can be safely said that the majority of physical fights are started *after* a heated verbal exchange of words. Very rarely do physical fights break out *before* some kind of insulting word or verbal challenge is made by one or both parties who are fighting. The fight usually begins with words.

In Proverbs 15:1, Solomon so wisely says, "A soft answer turns away wrath, but a harsh word stirs up anger." Both parts of this verse have been proved true over and over again throughout history.

The parking lot of my old gym has very little shade cover from the hot sun, with only a few trees in the whole lot. During the hot summer months in San Diego, most people, including myself, prefer a shaded parking spot. One morning, when I pulled into the parking lot at the gym, I starting heading for one of the only two shaded spots in the lot. When I arrived, I saw that a large, white van was parked right in the middle of both of the spots, taking all the shade and leaving no space for anyone else to park in either spot (which I later learned was intentional). Annoyed, I parked in one of the many sunny spots and went about my day. The next day, I pull into the gym parking lot and, guess what I find. The same van was parked in the same spot—or, *spots*—without leaving room for anyone else to have shade. This happened on several occasions until, finally, one day I wrote a very kind note, politely asking the driver to use only one of the shaded spots so that others could use the only other shaded spot in the lot. I stuck it on his windshield and went to work out. The driver apparently either didn't get the message or he simply didn't care because he continued his inconsiderate habit.

One day, annoyed yet again, I decided to teach him a lesson (I admit it, I was in the flesh, not walking in the Spirit). I parked obnoxiously close to his driver-side door. In order for me to open my door widely enough to get in and out of my car comfortably, I (gently) moved his mirror in, doing no harm to the car or mirror since the mirrors are made to be able to turn. Little did I know, the driver was standing on the other side of the parking lot talking to a friend and watching me. When he saw me touch his mirror, he exploded in anger. He started walking very quickly toward me, yelling at me and cussing me out, ready to fight. My adrenaline kicked in and I was ready to defend myself and throw down with this guy. I had been taking Jiu Jitsu for a while, so I was ready to go. But just before he reached me, a thought popped into my head (I wonder where it came from): "A soft answer turns away wrath, but a harsh word stirs up anger." By God's grace, I decided to put the first part of this verse into practice. With the guy six inches from my face, screaming and cursing at me and his saliva flying everywhere, I calmly de-escalated the situation, apologizing for touching his mirror, softly explaining my frustration with him, and politely asking him to use only one parking spot. And guess what happened! Exactly what Solomon said happened that day in that parking lot. After a minute, the dude chilled out and we became friendly acquaintances, saying hi to each other and giving a fist bump every day at the gym.

I wish I could say that there have been more times in my life where I put the first rather than the second part of Proverbs 15:1 into practice. I have proven the second part of the verse to be true many more times than I have the first part, but I'm working on it and, by God's grace, I'll continue to grow. What about you? Which part of Proverbs 15:1 do you find yourself utilizing more often: the soft answer or the harsh word?

When a lot of people get angry, whatever self-control they previously had over their mouth is now long gone, and as a result, they unleash a furious flurry of negative words intended for a single purpose: to hurt and destroy their target. How do you respond when someone insults you or is unkind to you with their words? Do you lash back with your words or do you follow the example of Christ, "who, when He was reviled, did not revile in return; when He suffered, He did not threaten, but committed Himself to Him who judges righteously?" (1 Pet. 2:23).

Though our natural inclination is to fire back with an offensive insult or to jab back with equally—or even fiercer—demeaning words, as Christians we're called to not follow our natural, fleshly impulses but to walk in the Spirit. Self-control is a fruit of the Spirit, and we need to remember that in situations when we're angry and tempted to unleash our wrathful words on others, we need to walk in the Spirit, exercise self-control, be slow to speak, and use a soft answer that turns away wrath. Other fruits of the Spirit that we should put into practice in such situations include love, patience, kindness, and gentleness (Gal 5:22-23). Furthermore, Jesus commands you to "love your enemies, bless those who curse you, do good to those who hate you, and pray for those who spitefully use you and persecute you" (Matt 5:44). How will the world see that we love and follow Jesus if we react to insults the same way as everyone else? If we're kind only to those who are kind to us, then we're no different than everyone else. Even worldly people do that. In order for the world to see Jesus in us, we need to respond to people the way Jesus did and the way He commanded us. Solomon says, "The words of a wise man's mouth *are* gracious" (Eccl 10:12). Therefore, we must do as Scripture commands us: "*Let* your speech always *be* with grace" (Col 4:6).

The Joker

When I was a high school teacher, I attended a graduation ceremony for some of my students. The young man who was the salutatorian went up to give his speech. In front of thousands of people, he made fun of a young man who was a fellow graduate by making a joke about his short stature and the fact that he was "small" compared to the rest of his class. Some people laughed. A lot didn't. I was infuriated at the one student and my heart wept for the other who had just been made the center of a heartless joke, a joke that was made at his own expense in front of so many people. For the graduate who was made fun of, it was thus far in life one of the biggest, most exciting days of his life, and one of the most climactic parts of that day and moment was totally ruined. A great day became a terrible day all because of someone's careless, *joking* words. How many times throughout his life had he been made fun of for his size, something over which he didn't even have control? You can bet that all those childhood experiences caused self-consciousness, embarrassment, and insecurities prior to that graduation ceremony, and you can bet that those few passing remarks made by his salutatorian crushed him and made those bad roots run even deeper. This young man will probably never forget that moment of humiliation, and will probably think of it most times he recalls his graduation night.

In Proverbs 26:18-19, Solomon remarks profoundly, "Like a madman who throws firebrands, arrows, and death, is the man who deceives his neighbor, and says, 'I was only joking!'" How many times have we been that madman who throws all kinds of hurtful words at people in the form of a joke, yet those words bring death to them? I personally tend to be a very sarcastic person. I love to joke around and make people laugh. Unfortunately, I often catch myself making others laugh by making fun of someone and doing so at his/her own expense. So often when we do this, we don't even think for a moment how our words and our joke might affect our targeted victim. We don't think before we speak. We just spout out what *we* think will make people laugh without giving any thought to how that one person will feel.

We all hate being made fun of by others at our own expense, and yet how often do we do it to others without giving it a second—or maybe even a first—thought. We care more about making *some* people laugh *for a mere moment* than we do about *one* person's feelings *for possibly a lifetime*. And why are we usually so focused on making people laugh? A lot of times it can be selfishly motivated; we want other people to view us in a certain way, namely, as being funny, witty, or intelligent. So, in our pursuit to gain attention, acceptance, and praise, we stomp on others and hurt them with our joking words.

The apostle Paul urges Christians to allow no "foolish talking, nor coarse jesting" to "even be named among you" (Eph 5:3-4). Now, does that mean Christians can never joke around with each other and have fun? No, it doesn't, but there is a line that we need to be careful not to cross, and sometimes it is difficult to know when you're crossing over than line and going too far. So, I urge you, be careful not to cross that line. It's better to err on the side of caution by keeping your mouth closed—so as to preserve someone's feelings and save them some unnecessary pain that your words might inflict on them—than to open your mouth and realize *afterward* that you crossed the line. You need to figure out where that boundary line is and, in the process, it's best to be slow to speak and have little or no regrets instead of speaking a lot and having many big regrets.

Gossip

A lot of people have a misunderstanding of what gossip truly is. First of all, gossip does not have to consist purely of lies about someone else. Though gossip oftentimes involves saying things about someone that either aren't true or are not yet confirmed to be true, it can also consist of telling true statements about that person. So then, if the core problem of gossip does not necessarily have to do with whether what is said is true or false, then what is the core issue?

Gossip can be a difficult word to define since it can encompass so much. Simply put, gossip is speaking about a person or people behind their back in a negative way that is not edifying, uplifting, or God-glorifying. In explaining the difference between gossip and flattery, author R. Kent Hughes writes, "Gossip involves saying behind a person's back what you would never say to his or her face. Flattery means saying to a person's face what you would never say behind his or her back."[43] There is a lot of profound truth to these words.

James 4:11 urges, "Do not speak evil of one another, brethren. He

---

[43] R. Kent Hughes, *Disciplines of a Godly Man* rev. ed. (Wheaton, IL: Crossway Books, 2001), 139.

who speaks evil of a brother and judges his brother, speaks evil of the law and judges the law. But if you judge the law, you are not a doer of the law but a judge."

Gossip has many effects. More often than not, gossip breeds bitterness and contempt in the hearts of those gossiping toward their target about whom they're gossiping. And as gossip oftentimes consists of rumors which aren't even true to begin with, those who are gossiping end up believing lies about that person and, in turn, viewing him/her in an unfair way, judging that person to be guilty of a crime which, in reality, he/she never even committed. An innocent person's reputation can be ruined because of gossiping lies which are told and then believed by people about that person and then spread to others.

Another effect of gossip is that it stirs up strife, contention, and division among people. Solomon counsels, "Where *there is* no wood, the fire goes out; and where *there is* no talebearer, strife ceases" (Prov 26:20). A talebearer is synonymous with a gossiper. The point is clear: if you get rid of a person who gossips, you'll be getting rid of all kinds of strife at the same time. Elsewhere Solomon says that "gossip separates the best of friends" (Prov 16:28 NLT). Gossip breeds division, and this is exactly what Satan wants. He loves dividing people, especially the people of God. And unfortunately, all too often, he is successful is making division a reality amongst Christians, and gossip is one of his tools he uses to accomplish this.

When we choose to use our tongues to gossip and rip apart the body of Christ, we're representing the heart of the Devil, not the heart of Christ. Gossip tears apart people who shouldn't be divided, and it makes ungodly alliances. In other words, it unites people (the gossipers) in an evil cause. One of the seven abominations to the Lord is a person "who sows discord among brethren" (Prov 6:19). Keep that in mind the next time you are tempted either to gossip or listen to gossip about someone else. Gossip only ever contributes to problems; it never solves them.

In his *Believer's Bible Commentary*, William MacDonald adds a striking quote about gossip that was found many years ago in the *Atlanta Journal*:

> I am more deadly than the screaming shell of a howitzer. I win without killing. I tear down homes, break hearts, and wreck lives. I travel on the wings of the wind. No innocence is strong enough to intimidate me, no purity pure enough to daunt me. I have no regard for truth, no respect for justice, no mercy for the defenseless. My victims are as numerous as the sands of the sea, and often as innocent. I never forget and seldom forgive. My name is Gossip.[44]

Beware the company you keep. If, when hanging around certain people, you tend to fall into the sin of gossip, it's time to make a change. Take a bold and courageous stand and shut the gossip down as soon as it starts. Tell the people gossiping that you won't listen to or participate in any gossip. If the person you're hanging out with refuses to stop gossiping, maybe it's time to distance yourself from him/her. Also, beware of the cop-out many Christians use when gossiping: *I'm telling you this so you can pray.* More often than not, many—not all—Christians use that statement as a means to justify their gossip. They have no true intention of praying and actually helping to solve the problem. Rather, they just want freedom from guilt and conviction to gossip, so they disguise their gossip by placing it under the cloak of explaining a prayer need. Watch out for that in others and in yourself!

Finally, remember Jesus' golden rule: do unto others as you would want them to do to you (Matt 7:12). Would you want the things that either you're saying or the things that you're hearing to be said

---

[44] William MacDonald, *Believer's Bible Commentary*, (Nashville, TN: Thomas Nelson Publishers, 1995), 858.

about you by others behind your back?

The big question, then, is how does one discern whether saying specific things is or isn't considered gossip? This is not an easy question to answer since there certainly are times when some things need to be spoken and communicated to others. Here are just a few guidelines to follow. First, Solomon warned, "In the multitude of words sin is not lacking, but he who restrains his lips *is* wise" (Prov 10:19). The more you speak, the better the chances that you will say something sinful. Therefore, if you're unsure whether saying a certain statement might fall into the category of gossip, then stop, restrain yourself from speaking, and pray for wisdom. It's better not to say something that you aren't sure is or isn't gossip than to say it and regret it later.

Second, examine the purpose and the content of the conversation at hand. For example, let's say you're upset at your friend Daniel, and you're considering confronting him. However, you aren't sure if you're just overreacting and you want to be wise about how you approach the situation. You go to your friend, Luke, who you trust to give you wise, godly, unbiased counsel and you explain the situation to him. So far, everything is good. The purpose of the conversation is God-honoring. However, let's say you get to a point in the conversation where, while explaining why you think Daniel is in the wrong, Luke chimes in and says, "Yeah, Daniel did that to me too. He's a jerk. He always does stuff like that. One time he…" Everything Luke is saying is only making you angrier at Daniel, and everything you continue to say only makes Luke feel the same way. Where is the conversation going now? What is the content of the conversation? And what is its purpose? At this point, is the purpose and content of the conversation edifying and God-glorifying? Nope. You guys are no longer looking for a biblical solution to your problem. Now, you're just engaging in verbal attacks on Daniel behind his back, furthering your division with and bitterness toward Daniel. Therefore, it's time to cut the conversation off or divert it back to its original purpose, if possible.

Now, let's tweak your conversation with Luke. Let's say you're asking him for advice and explaining to him the struggle you're having with Daniel. At this point, instead of joining in and complaining with you about Daniel, Luke listens and then gives good, godly counsel and also helps you to see where maybe you're in the wrong and need to change. This is excellent! We often need to seek counsel from others and get their feedback. God didn't create us to do the whole lone ranger thing. He created us for community, and we need each other. Solomon says that "in the multitude of counselors there is safety" (Prov 11:14; 24:6). Therefore, asking counsel of others when we're having problems with someone can be very beneficial and can help us see things we're missing. In fact, asking counsel of others is often a crucial part of being a wise Christian. But let me also add that a wise Christian is careful about the *type* of people they ask for counsel. Don't ask counsel of flatterers or yes men. Ask counsel of people who

- are serious about following Christ,
- will always take you back to Scripture and speak God's truth to you,
- will tell you what you *need* to hear and not necessarily what you *want* to hear,
- know you well and can see where you tend to be wrong and need growth and, are therefore, better equipped to help guide you.

Third, if you learn certain pieces of negative information about someone else, be very careful what you do with that knowledge. Solomon says, "The tongue of the wise uses knowledge rightly" (Prov 15:2). Therefore, don't use your knowledge you have about others to gossip about them. Use it wisely. Heed the words of Solomon yet again, "A talebearer reveals secrets, but he who is of a faithful spirit conceals a matter" (Prov 11:13). Don't go around spreading negative information about people to all your friends. A faithful person conceals information that won't be helpful to spread.

Filthy Language

Yet another way in which the tongue can be used for evil is through dirty language which can entail a lot (e.g., cursing, crude talk, explicit or sensual language, name-calling). Have you ever been around people who talked so dirty that you felt like you needed to take a shower afterward because you felt polluted? We are surrounded by a culture that esteems filthy language. So many of today's movies, TV shows, music, and celebrities promote this kind of talk. It is difficult to find a movie or TV show today that doesn't contain ample amounts of sexual innuendoes and crude humor. Our culture has become a place where filthy language is the norm. And yet Christians are called to be different from the world and its sinful habits, not to follow the norm but to be like Jesus.

We are commanded in Scripture to "present your bodies a living sacrifice, holy, acceptable to God, *which is* your reasonable service. And do not be conformed to this world, but be transformed by the renewing of your mind, that you may prove what *is* that good and acceptable and perfect will of God" (Rom 12:1-2). How do we do this? How do we live in such a way where we aren't conforming ourselves to the world but giving ourselves as an acceptable sacrifice to God? How do we live and look like Jesus rather than like the world? The answer, in part, is by our language. People can often tell when a person is a Christian—or, at least, different from the norm—by the way they talk—or, how they *don't* talk. We can live as acceptable sacrifices to God by obeying His Word, and His Word commands us to "rid yourselves of … filthy language from your lips" (Col 3:8 NIV) and to lay aside "all evil speaking" (1 Pet 2:1). This isn't an option for the Christian. If we claim to follow Christ then we must live as He lived. Furthermore, we're commanded, "Let no unwholesome word proceed from your mouth, but only such *a word* as is good for edification according to the need *of the moment,* so that it will give grace to those who hear" (Eph 4:29 NASB).

How do we discern what language is filthy and what is not? With some language it's blatantly clear that it's filthy. Other times, it can be more difficult to figure out. A good rule of thumb to follow is exactly what Paul instructed the Christians in the city of Thessalonica: "Abstain from every form of evil" (1 Thess 5:22). The *King James Version* uses the word *appearance* instead of *form.* The idea is that we should avoid any action or words that might even have the appearance of evil so that we might live above reproach in every way. By the way, if you have to ask whether saying some word or phrase or joke is inappropriate, the fact that you even need to ask in the first place might be a sign that you shouldn't say it. Once again, it's better not to speak if you aren't sure whether something is wrong to say than to speak and regret it later.

Self-Exaltation

In an attempt to make ourselves look great, we can oftentimes belittle and criticize others with our words while puffing ourselves up and boasting of our own achievements. Contrary to what might be expected, acting in this way hurts not only others, but it hurts ourselves as well. As will be discussed in chapter nine, God hates pride, and there are serious consequences for arrogantly exalting ourselves (1 Pet 5:5). Thus, by means of self-exaltation we harm ourselves and, in the process, we also hurt others because, well, obviously nobody likes being belittled or criticized.

Interestingly, sometimes an underscoring reason that a person belittles and makes fun of others is because of his/her own self-consciousness, insecurity, and embarrassment. This is especially true of a lot of bullies. They wear a mask, so to speak, to cover up their own insecurities and to keep people from seeing their true feelings. For example, people may put on the mask of appearing strong and tough, and will harm others verbally and/or physically for the purpose of covering up and hiding their own fear (or even possible shame and embarrassment) from being abused personally in their past.

> **Scenario #1**: Sarah has a lot of insecurities about some of her own bodily features, say, her physique or her body weight. She has been laughed at and made the center of jokes in the past because of these features and, understandably, she hates being made fun of by other people. To hide her insecurities and self-consciousness, Sarah makes fun of and criticizes the physical appearance or physique of other women. She may even argue that her body is more natural and that the women who look "good" are fake and must have gotten some kind of enhancements, reductions, enlargements, or other work done on their bodies because there's no way they could look that good naturally, or by using pure discipline to exercise. Though some her assumptions about other women may be true, the point is that Sarah belittles and tears them down as a means to cover up her own insecurities about her own body.

This happens more often than you may think.

> **Scenario #2**: Jeremy has a lot of self-consciousness about, say, his body type and size, his height, his athleticism, and/or other features. One of the reasons for these insecurities is because he has been made fun of or ridiculed by others for these things in the past. In an attempt to mask his self-consciousness and to give off the impression that he is strong and tough, Jeremy bullies people. He might do this through physical violence, or by use of his mouth. He belittles and attacks people by using his words to make fun of their size, body features, their small muscles, or their shortcomings in athletics. Some of the reasons Jeremy

does these things might include (1) to make himself feel better about his own body, (2) to try to cover up and keep people from seeing his own self-consciousness about his own body, or (3) because *he* gets made fun of for one or more of his own physical features and he wants to deflect people's attention away from joking about *him*, so he accomplishes this by getting people's attention on laughing at *someone else's* physique. If everyone is too busy laughing at and making fun of Jeremy's target, that means they won't be making fun of Jeremy. Jeremy doesn't want others to see his *own* flaws and then possibly make fun of him, so he tries to keep them distracted from *himself* by choosing a victim to make fun of.

These kinds of things happen much more often than you may think. It happens all the time in schools among immature teens and pre-teens, which is no surprise, but it happens quite frequently even among adults as well.

Oftentimes, but not always, people who go around tearing others down and exalting themselves usually do so because they're afraid, insecure, and very sensitive; and they think they have to prove something to everybody, namely, that they are strong, intelligent, great, beautiful, and so on. If this is true of you in any way, don't hurt others to "help" yourself. It's the opposite of what really happens. You don't actually help yourself in the long run. Also, such a spiteful attitude is contrary to the heart of God. If other people do these things to you, remember that it could be because of their own fear and insecurity. And show grace to them. Don't seek revenge against them. Rather, implement the heart and attitude of Christ by trying to help them experience restoration and healing.

Lying

Both Proverbs 6:17 and 12:22 say that lying is an abomination to the Lord. Furthermore, Jesus said that Satan is the father of lies (John 8:44). When you lie, you are harming both yourself and others. You're harming *yourself* by engaging in that which God hates, thus creating a barrier in your relationship with Him and inviting His discipline upon yourself. You're harming *others* by guiding them away from truth through deceiving and tricking them into believing something that is outside of reality. God does not treat lying lightly. Serious judgment awaits those who practice lying.

Deadly Poison

There is an interesting metaphor from nature about the tongue's destructive power.[45] Many female spiders do not possess a stomach and are, therefore, unable to digest the bodies of their victims who have the misfortune of getting trapped in their webs. Therefore, in order to eat a fly or other insect that is caught in her net, the spider will bite the fly and inject her poison into its body. The venom is so strong and deadly that, over time, it will turn the fly's insides into a warm liquid. She is then able to come and suck out the soupy liquid from the fly. The result is that the fly, who to the human eye *looks* alive, is actually a hollowed-out corpse. He is "a hollow casket" and the spider's "dinner room is a morgue."[46]

What is the connection to the tongue? Walter Wangerin says, "This soup she swills even as most of us swill souls of one another after having cooked them in various enzymes: guilt, humiliations, subjectivities, cruel love – there are a number of fine, acidic mixes. And some among us are so skilled with the hypodermic word that our dear ones continue to sit up and to smile, quite as though they were

---

[45] I am borrowing this metaphor from Hughes, who borrowed it from Walter Wangerin, Jr., *Ragman and Other Cries of Faith* (San Francisco, CA: Harper & Row, 1984), 26.

[46] Hughes, 138.

still alive."[47]

Just as the spider with her mouth destroys the inside of a fly and sucks out the life from it, so too our words can—and often do—pierce to people's hearts, destroy their souls, and suck out the life from them to the point that they look alive on the outside but are hollow and dead on the inside, all because of our words. Hughes rightly says, "This world is populated by walking human caskets because countless lives have been dissolved and sucked empty by another's words."[48] As a point of application, ask yourself, Am I contributing to this grave problem, or am I helping to heal it?

> *"The boneless tongue, so small and weak*
> *Can crush and kill," declares the Greek,*
> *"The tongue destroys a greater horde,"*
> *The Turk asserts, "than does the sword."*
> *The Persian proverb wisely saith,*
> *"A lengthy tongue – an early death!"*
> *Or sometimes takes this form instead,*
> *"Do not let your tongue cut off your head."*
> *"The tongue can speak a word whose speed,"*
> *Say the Chinese, "outstrips the steed."*
> *The Arab sages said in part,*
> *"The tongue's great storehouse is the heart."*
> *From Hebrew was the maxim sprung,*
> *"Thy feet should slip, but ne'er the tongue."*
> *The sacred writer crowns the whole,*
> *"Who keeps the tongue doth keep his soul."*[49]

---

[47] Wangerin, 26.

[48] Hughes, 138.

[49] James S. Hewitt, ed., *Illustrations Unlimited* (Wheaton, IL: Tyndale House Publishers, 1988), 475.

How to Self-Destruct

Using your tongue for evil in the ways discussed above will cause pain, destruction, and death to *other people*, but it'll also bring ruin to *your own life*. For example, tearing others down and gossiping will cause division and burn bridges between you and them, bridges that aren't meant to be burned. You will lose and greatly damage many relationships in your life with people whom you need. People tend to dislike those who are prideful and arrogant. If you habitually put others down and puff yourself up with your words, most people won't want to be your friend. Thus, you'll lose friends because of your haughty words, and you'll miss out on great relationships due to your lack of humility. When it comes to lying, not only do you lose all credibility and trust with people, but you also are choosing to live in a way that is abominable to God, which will surely cause your relationship with Him will suffer tremendously. Furthermore, Solomon says that a liar "will not go unpunished" (Prov 19:5). There are so many other ways that your tongue can ruin your life.

Your relationship with God is the most important thing in this world. If you choose to live a lifestyle of continuously using your tongue for these sinful purposes, then you'll be living at odds with God's will for your life. And if you live contrary to God's will for your life, you're living in the flesh and in sin, and there is no blessing to be had in that lifestyle. Rather, living in rebellion to God produces only ruin (Rom 8:5-8).

So, are you looking for effective ways to destroy your life and also ruin a lot of others' lives in the process? If so, then simply be quick to speak and make a habit of sinning with your mouth in any of the ways discussed above. Jesus said, "For by your words you will be justified, and by your words you will be condemned" (Matt 12:37). Remember that "the one who speaks foolishness will come to ruin" (Prov 10:8 NET) and "he who opens wide his lips shall have destruction" (Prov 13:3).

10

THE LIFE-SAVING ALTERNATIVE: DISCRETION

The fact that our mouths and tongues can be used for endless evil does *not* mean that we should never ever speak. Indeed, Solomon says that there is a time to speak and a time to be silent (Eccl 3:7). So then, we aren't supposed to live some kind of weird, ascetic life where we never speak. Rather, we simply need to be very careful about *how* and *what* we speak, as Paul commands us to "speak the truth in love" (Eph 4:15 NLT). Just as we learned in chapter four that we need to filter what comes *into* our lives because it will influence *us*, so we must also filter what goes *out of* our mouths because it will influence *others* (remember, your tongue has the power to bring death and life). Therefore, how do we filter what comes out of our mouths? The answer—and the life-saving alternative to destroying our lives via our mouths—is *discretion*.

The word *discreet* means, "To have or show a judicious reserve in one's speech or behavior; to show good judgment; to be careful and circumspect in one's speech or actions." The alternative to having a godless mouth is to have a wise mouth that practices discretion. Throughout this chapter we have examined several verses from Proverbs about the tongue, but we've examined only half of each of those verses—the negative part. Let's now examine the other half of each verse:

- "But he who restrains his lips *is* wise." Proverbs 10:19b
- "He who guards his mouth preserves his life." Proverbs 13:3a
- "The heart of the righteous studies how to answer." Proverbs 15:28a
- "The heart of the wise teaches his mouth, and adds learning to his lips." Proverbs 16:23
- "Whoever guards his mouth and tongue keeps his soul from troubles." Proverbs 21:23

All of these verses are speaking of exercising discretion and thinking before you speak. Wise people are very careful with how they speak. They make sure that both the content of their words and the way in which that content is delivered are godly. On the other hand, the foolish person is careless and indiscreet with his/her words. Upon thorough examination of what comes out of your mouth on a regular basis, which category describes you best, the wise person or the fool?

If you are someone who talks a lot and/or tends to say foolish things when you speak, I want to encourage and challenge you to practice something: *speak less*. My reason for saying this can be found in the following passages. Ecclesiastes 5:3 says that "a fool's voice *is known* by *his* many words." Proverbs 17:27-28 says, "He who has knowledge spares his words…. Even a fool is counted wise when he holds his peace; when he shuts his lips, *he is considered* perceptive." Though Proverbs 10:19 has already been quoted, it bears repeating: "In the multitude of words sin is not lacking, but he who restrains his lips is wise." All of these verses share a common theme, namely, that it is better to be wise and practice speaking less than to talk a lot and heighten the chances of saying something foolhardy that you'll regret and have to apologize for. I'm not saying you need to be weird and take some crazy vow of silence, but simply practice speaking less and, instead of speaking, spend more time practicing discretion.

An essential aspect of discretion is learning to filter your words and bridle your tongue.

Filters and Bridles

What is the purpose of a filter? As it relates to water, a filter sifts out the impurities and unclean elements while it brings in the good, clean water. Filters are a great necessity. Imagine going to the dentist and the assistant sprays the water from the tube into your mouth and you notice some dark streams in the tube and some disgusting liquid coming out of that tube and into your mouth. You ask what that stuff is, and they say, "Oops, some sewage leaked into our water" or, "Oh, it looks like some of the previous patient's blood and pus got stuck in the tube." Disgusting picture, I know, but that's just the point. You'd obviously be disgusted and would demand clean, *filtered* water. Well, it's not just our water that we desperately need to be filtered; our mouths also need a filter on them to prevent unwholesome words from coming out.

When I was in high school, my mouth got me into a lot of trouble. I would talk back a lot, tear people down with my words, sarcastically joke about them, and be unkind with my tongue. One day, and many times after that, my dad told me that I had "diarrhea of the mouth." Not only was I completely grossed out by that picture, I also wondered why he would say such a thing. But then I got to thinking about what he meant and then it all made sense. When I wouldn't filter my words but would instead let filthiness spew out of my mouth, it was like nasty, disgusting diarrhea coming out of my mouth. Words of unkindness, rebellion, and rudeness that I would speak had the same—or worse—effect as when people think of diarrhea: disgust.

We all know people who have no filter when it comes to the things they say. Because of their lack of such a filter, they often get into a lot of trouble, they hurt and offend a lot of people, and they have to do a lot of apologizing for things they've said. As a word of advice, don't be that kind of person. Solomon says, "A fool vents all his feelings" (Prov 29:11). In other words, the fool has no filter. He always speaks whatever is on his mind and never practices restraint. This is a horrible and dangerous way to live. Each one of us desperately needs to filter the words that come out of our mouths.

Let's go back to the epistle of James for a brief moment. In James 1:26, we are told, "If anyone among you thinks he is religious, and does not bridle his tongue but deceives his own heart, this one's religion *is* useless." Those are some striking, sobering words. James is saying that if you claim to be a dedicated follower of Jesus and to be religiously pious but don't control your tongue, your so-called spirituality is a joke. Hughes wisely says, "An out-of-control tongue suggests bogus religion, no matter how well one's devotion is carried out" and, "The true test of a man's spirituality is not his ability to speak … but rather his ability to bridle his tongue."[50] Think of how profound a point this is. One of the earmarks of true, God-glorifying religion is the bridling of the tongue. And yet how many churches are filled with Christians who devote little—if any—of their time and energy on practicing and growing in this godly virtue?

I'll finish this chapter with giving you three steps to take, with the end goal of learning to filter your words and bridle your tongue, so that you become more like Christ in being a man or woman of discretion to the glory of God. Put these three steps into practice on a daily basis and, with the gracious help of the Holy Spirit, you're guaranteed to grow in having a more filtered mouth and a bridled tongue. And in doing so, you'll become more like Christ and become a more effective witness to the world.

---

[50] Hughes, 142.

Step 1: Heart Change

How do we learn to bridle our tongues and filter what comes out of our mouths? Well, we need to start by going to the root of the problem. In Matthew 12:34, Jesus said that "out of the abundance of the heart the mouth speaks." The *New American Standard Bible* reads, "For the mouth speaks out of that which fills the heart." Later, in Matthew 15:18, Jesus would say, "But those things which proceed out of the mouth come from the heart, and they defile a man." So then, the first step toward bridling your tongue is that your heart needs to be radically changed. That may seem impossible to you but, thankfully, God is in the business of changing hearts. In fact, you cannot change your own heart in your own strength. You desperately need to rely on the Spirit to help make that change happen. So, ask God for help. An excellent prayer you can offer to God is David's prayer for discretion, "Set a guard, O LORD, over my mouth; keep watch over the door of my lips" (Ps 141:3). In addition to praying for a changed heart, immerse yourself in God's Word and allow Him to convict you, change you, and wash you in the water of His Word (Eph 5:26). For, "The law of the LORD *is* perfect, converting the soul" (Ps 19:7).

Step 2: The Golden Rule

Have you ever thought about how difficult it is to be mindful of every one of God's commands to the Christian found in the New Testament, and to obey them every day? It can be a bit overwhelming when you consider just how many commands there are in the New Testament, especially since as humans we're so forgetful. But consider this: so many of God's commands to us can be summed up in Jesus' golden rule that He gave to His followers in Matthew 7:12, which says, "Therefore, whatever you want men to do to you, do also to them, for this is the Law and the Prophets." Consider something: if we, for one whole day or week, focused only on obeying this one command of Jesus (I'm not encouraging you to ignore His other commands) to treat others the way we want to be treated, that alone would be extremely difficult and would be so time-consuming. But think of the effect it could have.

My point is this: sometimes we can get overwhelmed because we want to obey God but we realize that there are so many commands in Scripture and we can't remember all of them every moment of the day. But what if, instead of constantly trying to remember every single command to obey, you spent a whole week seriously analyzing yourself and keeping yourself in check regarding what you've read in this chapter about your words? What if your sole focus was only on glorifying God and edifying others with your mouth rather than tearing people down? That would take a ton of work, but think of how much good it could do. Two other commands you can constantly consider before you speak are what Jesus called the two greatest commandments: love God and love others (Matt 22:34-40). Anytime you speak, before those words come out of your mouth, ask yourself, "Are the words I'm about to speak honoring to God and loving to others?" If not, keep your trap shut. I bet that if you seriously tried for one whole week to constantly focus intently on following Jesus' golden rule and treating others the way you want to be treated, a lot of good would come from it. People would see a good reflection of Christ in you and they'd be edified. You'd also recognize a major positive change in your own life. And your actions would be contagious.

Step 3: THINK

We sin with our words so much more than we realize. So, I have yet another challenge for you: spend the entire next week, starting now, acting as a metaphorical metal detector with your words. Don't let anything come out of your mouth that won't glorify God and edify others. In fact, here's an acronym for how you can detect whether or not you should speak in any given moment: THINK.

True: is what I'm about to say *true?*

Helpful: is what I'm about to say *helpful?*

Inspiring: is what I'm about to say *inspiring* in a good way?

Necessary: is what I'm about to say *necessary?*

Kind: is what I'm about to say *kind?*

If what you're about to say doesn't fit with every part of the acronym, then don't say it. Do as James tells us and be slow to speak. You'll find that more often than not, people tend to regret far more what they *did say* than what they chose *not* to say. So what if you end up *not saying* a joke or a humorous comment to your friends about someone that might or might not hurt that person's feelings? Sure, people won't laugh or think you're hilarious, but maybe you will have saved someone else from being deeply hurt on the inside. Which is worth more? And when you answer that question, remember the golden rule. How would *you* want to be treated in that situation?

A Final Thought

In connection with my challenge to you in the THINK acronym, I encourage you to ponder Philippians 4:8, wherein Paul says, "Finally, brethren, whatever things are true, whatever things *are* noble, whatever things *are* just, whatever things *are* pure, whatever things *are* lovely, whatever things *are* of good report, if *there is* any virtue and if *there is* anything praiseworthy—meditate on these things." As you apply this verse to your life, don't only meditate on these things, but add in the words, *speak these things*. So then, speak only things that are true, noble, and so on. You'll find—and others will, too—that as you do this, your life will change in many wonderful ways, God will be honored by you, and people will be blessed by you. What if every single person in the world practiced this verse all the time? How different our world would be! To quote a line from that old Christmas song, "What a wonderful world this would be!"

Do you remember the verse from earlier in this chapter, that there is power in your tongue to bring death to people? Well, the verse also says that *life* is in the power of your tongue. You have the power to speak life and to use your mouth to help, build up, and bless people on a daily basis. "The mouth of the righteous is a fountain of life" (Prov 10:11 NASB) and "A wholesome tongue *is* a tree of life" (Prov 15:4). Just as there is an incredible amount of power to ruin others with your tongue, so also there is the same amount of power to use your tongue for good to bring life to people. The choice is yours.

Unfortunately, not everyone in the world *does* practice, on a daily basis, speaking only words that are true, pure, lovely, and such. In fact, few do. But what if even just *some* people did? They would then influence others in their own circle to do the same, who would then influence others in *their* own circles to do the same, and so on. And here's the thing: you can do the same thing. If you want to see serious change with the way people talk, the change must start with you. So then, do it!

11

DESPISING THE WORD

He who despises the word will be destroyed,
But he who fears the commandment will be rewarded.

Proverbs 13:13

The 18th century French philosopher Voltaire had a pretty low view of the Bible. Though he appreciated certain stories and sections of Scripture, it's pretty safe to say that Voltaire despised the Bible. In his *Philosophical Dictionary*, Voltaire wrote, "The Bible. That is what fools have written, what imbeciles commend, what rogues teach and young children are made to learn by heart."[51] Voltaire avidly attacked the reliability and historicity of the Bible, as well as many of its fundamental doctrines. He also said, "To invent all those things [in the Bible], the last degree of rascality. To believe them, the extreme of brutal stupidity."[52] In one of his books titled, *La Bible Enfin Expliquée* (The Bible Finally Explained), Voltaire wrote

---

[51] Voltaire as quoted in Daniel Merritt, "Voltaire's Prediction, Home, and the Bible Society: Truth or Myth? Further Evidence of Verification," CrossExamined.org, August 18, 2019, accessed November 17, 2020, https://crossexamined.org/voltaires-prediction-home-and-the-bible-society-truth-or-myth-further-evidence-of-verification/#_ftnref3.

[52] Ibid., https://crossexamined.org/voltaires-prediction-home-and-the-bible-society-truth-or-myth-further-evidence-of-verification/#_ftnref3.

that "the popes who forbade the reading of the Bible were extremely wise."[53] Clearly, Voltaire despised the Bible.

Ironically, it has been said that Voltaire predicted in 1776 that within 100 years, the Bible would be altogether extinct from the world, except for a copy that might be preserved in a museum for someone to see. The ironic thing is that within 50 years of Voltaire's death, his house was purchased by a pastor and it was turned into a Bible Society where Bibles and Gospel pamphlets were both printed and stored.[54] What did such an attitude of despising God's Word do for—or, rather, *to*—Voltaire in the end? Well, think of where Voltaire is today and where he will forever spend eternity.

In contrast to Voltaire, some of America's Founding Fathers held the Bible in very high esteem, and they recognized the essential role it must play in our lives and society. For example, John Jay, who served as the very first chief justice of the United States, wrote in a letter to his son, Peter, on April 8, 1784, "The Bible is the best of all books, for it is the Word of God and teaches us the way to be happy in this world and in the next. Continue therefore to read it and to regulate your life by its precepts."[55] John Adams, signer of the *Declaration of Independence* and the second president of the United States, in a letter to Thomas Jefferson on Christmas Day, 1813, said that he himself had investigated many religions and that the conclusion he came to in the matter is that "the Bible is the best book in the world."[56] Elias Boudinot was yet another Founding

---

[53] Voltaire as quoted in Nicholas Cronk, *The Cambridge Companion to Voltaire* (Cambridge: Cambridge University Press, 2009), 199.

[54] Ibid., https://crossexamined.org/voltaires-prediction-home-and-the-bible-society-truth-or-myth-further-evidence-of-verification/#_ftnref3.

[55] John Jay, *John Jay: The Winning of the Peace. Unpublished Papers 1780-1784*, ed. Richard B. Morris (New York, NY: Harper & Row Publishers, 1980), 709.

[56] John Adams, "*The Works of John Adams, vol. 10 (Letters 1811-1825, Indexes)* [1854]," Online Library of Liberty, accessed November 17,

Father who greatly revered the Bible and whose achievements in life were quite impressive, a couple of them being that he was the president of Congress and a signer of the Treaty of Paris. Boudinot wrote:

> For nearly half a century have I anxiously and critically studied that invaluable treasure [the Bible]; and I still scarcely ever take it up that I do not find something new – that I do not receive some valuable addition to my stock of knowledge or perceive some instructive fact never observed before. In short, were you to ask me to recommend the most valuable book in the world, I should fix on the Bible as the most instructive both to the wise and ignorant. Were you to ask me for one affording the most rational and pleasing entertainment to the inquiring mind, I should repeat, it is the Bible; and should you renew the inquiry for the best philosophy or the most interesting history, I should still urge you to look into your Bible. I would make it, in short, the Alpha and Omega of knowledge.[57]

Noah Webster, the writer of the very first American dictionary, said, "The moral principles and precepts *found in the Scriptures* [emphasis added] ought to form the basis of all our civil constitutions and laws."[58] He also said, "All the... evils which men suffer from vice, crime, ambition, injustice, oppression, slavery and war, proceed from their despising or neglecting the precepts contained in the Bible."[59] Furthermore, Webster commented, "The Bible is the chief moral cause of all that is good and the best corrector of all that is evil in human society – the best book for regulating the

---

2020, https://oll.libertyfund.org/titles/adams-the-works-of-john-adams-vol-10-letters-1811-1825-indexes.

[57] Elias Boudinot, *The Age of Revelation, or the Age of Reason Shewn to be An Age of Infidelity* (Philadelphia, PA: Asbury Dickins, 1801), xv.

[58] Noah Webster, *History of the United States* (New Haven, CT: Durrie & Peck, 1832), 339.

[59] Ibid., 339.

temporal concerns of men, and the *only book* that can serve as an infallible guide to future felicity."[60] There is a very clear distinction between Voltaire and these Founding Fathers when it comes to their stances on the Bible. One despised it, the others revered it.

Enough can't be said about the importance and the consequences of a person's attitude toward God's Word. For, the Bible is not just any Book. It's the very Word of God, His divine revelation to people. In it, God has revealed to us who He is, what He's like, who we are, what He has done for us, how we can obtain eternal life, and how He wants us to live. In God's Word we are also warned about what will lead to a person's doom. A person's reverence or rejection of this Book will, in so many ways, determine their destiny. In this chapter we'll explore (1) what it means and looks like, practically speaking, to despise the Word of God, (2) why doing so is totally destructive to one's life, and (3) the life-saving alternative that Solomon gives as a means to save ourselves from ruin.

Defining *Despising*

Solomon tells of a surefire way to destroy your life: despise God's Word. What does it mean, though, to despise something? The dictionary defines *despise* in this way: "to regard with contempt or disdain." Contempt and disdain are words that are not as frequently used today as in the past, so let's examine their definitions as well. *Contempt* means to have or to show open disrespect or willful disobedience to someone or something, to view something as beneath your consideration, or to view something as worthless or deserving of scorn. *Disdain* means to consider something unworthy of yourself because you are superior to it and, therefore, to reject it with scorn. Understanding these words gives us a fuller view of what it

---

[60] Ibid., *The Holy Bible, Containing the Old and New Testaments, in the Common Version, With Amendments of the Language* (New Haven, CT: Durrie & Peck, 1833), v.

truly means to despise God's Word: it is to (1) regard His Word as beneath yourself or your consideration, (2) regard it as unworthy of your attention, reverence, and obedience, and (3) show disrespect and willful disobedience toward it. The idea behind the Hebrew word used in Proverbs 13:13 for *despise* is to trample something with your feet. Thus, to despise God's Word is like metaphorically trampling on the Bible.

It should be noted that there are generally two things involved when someone despises something: *attitude* and *action*. Despising God's Word begins with the attitude—or perspective or view-point—of your heart and mind. Then, it moves to the action(s) of *rejecting* or *neglecting* God's Word. So, it begins in the heart and then eventually moves to your actions. (No wonder Solomon warned, "Keep your heart with all diligence" [Prov 4:23].)

Solomon clearly states that whoever views (attitude) and treats (action) God's Word in such a way will be destroyed. Why is this so? In order to answer this question accurately, it's important to first lay the groundwork by examining two preliminary issues: what God's Word *is* and what God's Word *does*. In other words, by having a good-working knowledge of both the nature and purpose or role of the Bible in our lives, we'll better understand why—and in what ways—despising it is so destructive. Therefore, let's explore two questions: (1) *Why* does despising God's Word destroy one's life? (2) *How* does despising God's Word destroy one's life? We'll answer the first question by examining what God's Word *is*, and we'll answer the second question by examining what God's Word *does* or *accomplishes*.

What God's Word *Is*

The Bible isn't merely an ancient book written thousands of years ago, nor is it just like any other book. Rather, it's the very Word of the living God who is omniscient (all-knowing) and all-wise.[61] God, who knows all things from beginning to end and in whom is sourced all knowledge and wisdom (Col 2:3), has chosen to reveal Himself to mankind in a variety of ways. One of these ways is through His written Word, the Bible. In this Book, God has revealed to mankind many crucial things that are incredibly important for them to know. In sum, the Bible is God's divine revelation to humans. Now, God never wastes words. Therefore, if God has seen fit to reveal Himself and His plan in His Word, then it is of utmost importance for people to know what is written therein and to then obey it. So, just what kinds of important things does the Bible divinely reveal to mankind? The answer is seemingly endless things, but let me mention just a few. The Bible is divine revelation of *what*?

Who God is

One of the main purposes of our existence as humans is to know God. Therefore, true life and true fulfillment in life is found in knowing Him. Therefore, if we despise God's written revelation of Himself, we're ripping ourselves off from fulfilling our purpose in life, and from living truly fulfilled lives. God's Word is one of the greatest sources for learning how to better know Him and who He is. Hence, one of the consequences of despising the Bible is to adopt a terrible ignorance about God. In fact, there is a direct connection in Hosea 4:1 and 6 between people despising God's Word and, therefore, becoming ignorant about Him, which destroys their

---

[61] While it is not within the scope of this book to apologetically defend and argue for the reliability, authority, and divine inspiration of the Bible, there are many excellent resources to which I will refer the reader for further study on these issues. For example, see Norman L. Geisler and William E. Nix, *A General Introduction To The Bible* (Chicago, IL: Moody Press, 1986). See also Norman Geisler, *Christian Apologetics*, 2nd ed. (Grand Rapids, MI: Baker Academic, 2013). See also online resources such as alwaysbeready.com, CARM.org, and crossexamined.org.

lives. Also, the person who worships God while despising His Word is destined to worship Him wrongly[62] and to form beliefs and ideas about Him that do not fit with reality.

How to Know God

As a result of sin, people's relationships with God have been tarnished. However, God reveals in His Word how that relationship can be restored and how mankind can know Him personally. Jesus defined eternal life beautifully: "And this is eternal life, that they may know You, the only true God, and Jesus Christ whom You have sent" (John 17:3). Eternal life is the renewal of a ruined relationship with God. It's knowing God personally. The Bible reveals in the words of Jesus not only how eternal life has been made possible for us but also what we must do to receive it: "For God so loved the world that He gave His only begotten Son, that whoever believes in Him should not perish but have everlasting life" (John 3:16).

Not only does the Bible divinely reveal how to know God in the sense of eternal life, but it also reveals how we can continually grow in gaining a deeper knowledge of God on a daily basis

---

[62] Yes, it is possible to worship God in a wrong way. In other words, a person may be passionate about worshiping God but may still go about doing so in ways that are displeasing to Him and contrary to the pattern that He laid out in His Word. Take, for example, the worship of offering sacrifices in the Old Testament. God told the Israelites that when they entered the Promised Land, they were not to choose just any place to offer sacrifices in their worship to God (Deut 12:5, 11, 14, 18, 26; 16:2). There was only one place they were permitted to offer sacrifices to God and that was in Jerusalem (1 Kgs 21:7). Unfortunately, many of the Israelites dishonored God by offering sacrifices *to Him* in many other places than at the temple in Jerusalem. They were still worshiping God, but they were worshiping Him wrongly in a manner that was not pleasing to Him. We, too, will experience the same consequences of worshiping God in ways that are not at all in line with His pattern laid out in the Bible if we choose to despise and neglect His Word.

throughout our life on earth. It's vital for a Christian to learn how to grow daily in his/her personal relationship with God because it's for this reason that we exist, namely, to know Him. How, as Christians, do we get to know God better? Thankfully, through His Word God has revealed to us exactly how to do this. The more we know God's Word, the better we'll know how to grow in our walk with Him, and the more we grow in our walk with Him, the more like Christ we'll become. (Think of what the alternative—despising God's Word—will produce in one's life.)

How People Should Live

The Bible reveals how a person must live in order to please and honor God. There are countless passages in Scripture that instruct us how to obey God and live a life that is well-pleasing to Him (e.g., 1 Thess 4:3; 5:18; Heb 11:6). God didn't give us commands in His Word for us to treat them as mere advice or suggestions. He gave them to us to obey because this is His desire for our lives. And to live within the boundaries of God's commands is the safest place for us to be. Despising God's Word, on the other hand, will inevitably cause us to live outside the protective boundaries He has set for us. To live this way is to walk down a dangerous road that leads only to destruction.

Why Does it Matter?

Now, there are many differing beliefs and opposing viewpoints in the world today about who God is, what He's like, how to know Him, how to honor and please Him, and so on. The Bible serves as our ruler or standard by which we measure various beliefs and claims made by people concerning these issues. If someone despises and rejects God's Word, then what standard does he/she use to form beliefs about these crucial issues? One of the most common standards people tend to use is their own opinions. When people reject God's Word and, instead, rely on their own opinions to form beliefs (which then lead to actions) about these important questions of life, they're guaranteed to be deceived and adopt false, unbiblical beliefs and ideas. Their beliefs and ideas about God will be distorted, their beliefs regarding sin, salvation and knowing God will be warped, and their concept of how to live to please and honor God will be tainted. Why? The reason is because they have despised God's divine revelation that provides exact answers of truth to each of these issues. Rightly did Solomon say, "There is a way that seems right to a man, but its end *is* the way of death" (Prov 14:12; 16:25). When people follow their own opinions instead of God's Word, they're headed down a road that leads to death and destruction.

To answer our question of *why* despising God's Word will destroy you, ponder this daunting reality: to reject God's Word is to reject truth (John 17:17), and if you reject truth, you'll be deceived by believing and living a lie, and that path leads only to destruction. To despise God's Word is to despise God Himself. And to despise God is to destroy one's own life.

Consider how foolish and arrogant the person is who despises God's Word: he's saying, in essence, that he—a small, sinful, terribly flawed, helpless, ignorant creature who knows almost nothing compared to all that can possibly be known—knows better than the all-wise, all-knowing, all-powerful, eternal God of the universe.

What's God's Word *Does*

To answer our second question of *how* despising the Bible destroys a person's life, let's examine the work that God's Word *does*—or, the role that it plays in a person's life—and then simply apply the opposite to the life of a person who rejects it. For example, if God's Word gives freedom, then to reject God's Word is to reject freedom and to receive the opposite, namely slavery. The following is brief list of some of the things that God's Word does or accomplishes:

- It gives life (Ps 119:50).
  - Therefore, to despise the Word is to reject life and receive death.
- It teaches, rebukes, corrects, and instructs in the ways of righteousness (2 Tim 3:16).
  - Therefore, to despise the Word is to reject good instruction and necessary rebuke and correction and to receive foolish counsel and yes-men who will not truly help you.
- It equips the Christian to be mature and complete (2 Tim 3:17).
  - Therefore, to despise the Word is to reject spiritual maturity and receive a character and lifestyle of immaturity and foolishness.
- It heals (Ps 107:20).
  - Therefore, the despise the Word is the refuse spiritual healing and to receive spiritual decay.
- It strengthens and builds up (Ps 119:28).
  - Therefore, to despise the Word is to reject strength from God, and to therefore be weak against the attacks of the enemy.
- It saves the soul (Jas 1:21).
  - Therefore, to despise the Word is to embrace the destruction of your soul.
- It gives liberty and freedom (Jas 1:25; 2:12).[63]
  - Therefore, to despise the Word is to embrace spiritual enslavement.

---

[63] Also combine John 17:17 with John 8:32.

- It is a guide to Jesus and to salvation (Gal 3:24; 2 Tim 3:15).
  - o Therefore, to despise the Word is to, in the case of the unbeliever, reject the way to life.
- It comforts (Ps 119:50).
  - o Therefore, to despise the Word is to reject help, comfort, and encouragement.
- It revives (Ps 119:25).
  - o Therefore, to despise the Word is to waste away and become drained of spiritual life and vigor.
- It upholds (Ps 119:116).
  - o Therefore, to despise the Word is to rely on your own strength, which will cause you to slip and be unstable.
- It sanctifies (John 17:17).
  - o Therefore, to despise the Word is to reject your spiritual growth, to refuse to be conformed into the image of Jesus, and to be a very poor witness and ambassador for Christ.
- It washes and cleanses (Eph 5:26; Ps 119:9).
  - o Therefore, to despise the Word is to reject spiritual cleansing and to embrace the pollution of sin.
- It leads in right ways and protects (Prov 6:22).
  - o Therefore, to despise the Word is to reject God's ways and to blaze your own dangerous trail.
- It is a lamp and a light to guide in dark places (Ps 119:105; Prov 6:23).

- o Therefore, to despise the Word is to walk blindly in darkness.
- It gives great peace to those who love it (Ps 119:165).
  - o Therefore, to despise the Word is to reject the peace of God and embrace chaos, worry, fear, frustration, and anxiety.
- It gives wisdom and understanding (Ps 119:169; 2 Tim 3:15).
  - o Therefore, to despise the Word is to reject wisdom and to choose foolishness and stupidity.
- It delivers (Ps 119:170).
  - o Therefore, to despise the Word is to reject God's deliverance and to rely on that which is a futile help.
- It guards and protects from sin (Ps 119:11).
  - o Therefore, to despise the Word is to open the door to sin.

How does despising God's Word destroy your life? To despise it is to shun and forsake these good things God has for you and to adopt their opposites, which lead to destruction.

Proverbs 28:9 tells us another way in which despising the Word is destructive: "One who turns away his ear from hearing the law, even his prayer *is* an abomination." The person who turns away from and forsakes God's Word clearly doesn't have an attitude of respect or reverence for it. Rather, that person despises it, and there are fearful consequences of doing so, namely, that his/her prayers will be abominable to God. In other words, you despise God's Word, and God will despise your prayer. Thus, despising the Word has a profoundly negative effect on one's prayer life and relationship with God.

Solomon gives yet further insight to this issue in Proverbs 19:16 when he says, "He who keeps the commandment keeps his soul, but he who is careless of his ways will die." The *New Living Translation* renders this verse, "Keep the commandments and keep your life; despising them leads to death." Notice the contrast here. The person who obeys God's Word protects his/her own soul. In contrast, the careless person will die. Do you see the implication here? The person who obeys God's Word isn't careless but is careful with how he/she lives, whereas a person who *doesn't* live in obedience to God's Word is therefore careless of his/her own ways. One of the fruits of despising God's Word is the adoption of a careless attitude toward your own actions and lifestyle. And Solomon foretells where having such a careless, reckless attitude will lead, namely to death. So, Solomon kindly gives you an easy recipe for disaster and an easy way to destroy your life: simply despise God's Word and be careless of your ways.

The *How-To's* of Despising God's Word

Now that we have both a good-working definition of what it *means* to despise God's Word, as well as some reasons *why* and *how* doing this is so destructive, let's now consider the *how-to's*—so to speak—of despising His Word. In other words, how does one despise the Word? What does that look like, practically speaking?

Despising God's Word can take many different forms. We'll start with the most obvious and then move toward the more subtle ways.

Outright, Blatant Abhorrence

Possibly one of the most obvious ways in which a person can despise God's Word is through showing outright disgust, ridicule, and rejection of it. This kind of attitude is perhaps most obviously descriptive of many atheists, who take joy in attacking the Bible's reliability, authenticity, ethical teachings and values, and so on. Atheists like Richard Dawkins claim that the Bible was written by a bunch of iron-age peasants.[64] Atheist philosopher Sam Harris claims that any book (and he does mean *any*) in Barnes & Noble will have more relevance and wisdom for the 21st century than does the Bible.[65] So then, the most obvious way to despise the Word is to express public, verbal, and even physical ridicule, disdain, and reproach for it.

Other people who might show an outright rejection of God's Word are secular humanists. Secular humanists are those who believe that the whole purpose of existence is for mankind to experience pleasure. "Do whatever makes you happy" is the gospel of the humanist. Well, the Bible preaches quite a different way of life and ethical standards. Therefore, it shouldn't be surprising that the humanist despises the Bible because it gives us rules, it commands us to live in a specific way, and it holds us accountable for our sinful actions.

Not Full Rejection, But Rejection of What I Don't Like

Maybe you're not an atheist or a secular humanist, so you might be thinking that you're in the clear regarding despising God's Word. Not so fast. Another way in which you can despise God's Word is by not completely, but only partially, rejecting it. In other words,

---

[64] Richard Dawkins, *The God Delusion* (New York, NY: Mariner Books, 2008), 268. For an example of atheist Sam Harris making the same claim, see Sam Harris, "The God Debate II: Harris vs. Craig," Youtube.com, April 12, 2011, accessed June 23, 2020, https://www.youtube.com/watch?v=yqaHXKLRKzg.

[65] Sam Harris, "Sam Harris: On Interpreting Scripture," Youtube.com, accessed June 23, 2020, https://www.youtube.com/watch?v=8zV3vIXZ-1Y. Harris' thinking is seriously flawed here. He is committing the logical fallacy of a hasty generalization.

you accept the parts of the Bible that you like and that fit with your worldview and you reject the parts that don't line up with your beliefs and lifestyle.

There is no shortage of people who view the Bible in such a way. For example, there are people—I had a former student like this—who say they are Christians and they claim that the Bible is God's Word, yet they believe that practices like abortion and homosexuality are morally okay even though they know Scripture clearly says they are morally wrong (e.g., Ps 139:13-16; 1 Cor 6:9). Are these people esteeming or despising God's Word when they knowingly choose to believe and proclaim that sinful practices as described in the Bible are actually okay? Rather than revering God's Word and conforming their beliefs to its standards, they're despising the Word by deliberately holding beliefs that they know are contrary to its teachings.

Other people—Christians and non-Christians alike—sift through the Bible and pick and choose what they want to believe and they reject whatever doesn't suit their own desires and lifestyles. I was walking through a mall in San Diego one night sharing the Gospel with people when I got into a discussion with a little old granny who I assumed would be sweet, like grandmas usually tend to be. I was dead wrong. As I was sharing the Gospel with her, the topic of Hell obviously came up, being that this is a significant part of the Gospel message and the place from where Jesus saved us spending eternity. Well, she blew up in my face and started yelling at me, saying, "I don't believe that Hell is real. *My* God would *never* send anyone to Hell." If you know anything about the Bible, you know that it clearly teaches that Hell is a real place to where unrepentant sinners will spend eternity after death. So, what was the problem? There was obviously some kind of disconnect between this woman's theology and what the Bible actually says. Our conversation revealed that she possessed an attitude of disdain for God's Word by saying that her belief—which was directly contrary to the Bible's teachings—was true and, in effect, was saying that God's Word is wrong. She was esteeming her own opinion above the very Word of God. To do so is to despise God's Word, and you'd be surprised how often we all do this.

The Subtler Ways to Despise the Word

At this point you might be thinking, "Perfect! I'm good. I don't fit into the above categories because I'm a *true* Christian. I *actually* believe the Bible is God's Word. I don't despise it. I'm good to go!" If this is true, great!

But wait one second. You're not off the hook quite yet. The age-old saying rings ever true, namely that actions speak louder than words. Therefore, when examining yourself and asking whether you despise God's Word, don't limit *despising the Word* to only the ways that I have mentioned above. Rather, ask yourself deeper, more pointed questions. For example, in what ways can you, a *Christian*, despise God's Word? Is it even possible, in the first place, for Christians to despise the very book upon which they claim that their entire faith is built? Let's find out.

The Hebrew word used for *despise* in Proverbs 13:13 has several meanings. One of those meanings is "to hold as insignificant." Remember, actions speak louder than words. We can *say* that we believe the Bible is God's Word and that it is, therefore, incredibly important and significant to us, but the true test is whether we *live* like it. Do your actions reflect a reverence for the Word of God? Maybe you're asking, "I'm not sure. How can I tell?" Well, ask yourself: what is your relationship like with the Bible?

If something is very near and dear to your heart, you hold it close. If you receive a letter from a loved one, you read it and cherish it. If a wise leader that you esteem highly writes a message to you, giving you important instructions to follow, you intently study every word. We treat these types of things very seriously, and our actions reveal the level of value and significance we place upon them.

One of the ways that we, Christians, can despise God's Word is by minimizing its significance and the important role it plays in our lives and in our spiritual growth. In what ways can we do this? There are many, but let me mention just a few.

Neglect

First, you can minimize the significance of God's Word in your life by *neglecting* it. Let it sit on the shelf and collect dust while you put off studying what's written inside it. Maybe you use the lame excuse that you're too busy and just don't have enough time to read the Word every day. But consider something: there are an entire 24 hours in a day. The average person spends about seven to nine (maybe more for some of you) of those hours sleeping. A lot of people spend about another eight or so hours of those 24 doing important things like working, commuting, going to school, eating, and so on. That's a lot of time in one day. How is the rest of that time spent? That depends on the person, but a lot of people spend a good chunk of that remaining time watching movies or TV, playing games, surfing through social media, reading a book, or doing other things they enjoy. What amount of time do we give to studying God's Word on a daily basis? How high of a priority is it in our lives? Are we not able to sacrifice a little bit of sleep to delve into the rich mines of God's Word to obtain eternal treasures found therein? Can we not give up some of the time we spend looking at the TV screen or staring aimlessly at our phones for communing with God in His Word, which is something that we claim to be of great significance to us? Is spending time studying the Word more of a burden to you than it is a joy?

A point of clarification is important here. My point in the above paragraph is not that having fun playing a game or watching a movie are morally wrong in and of themselves and that you should be spending every moment of your free time reading the Bible. My point is simply that we give time to the things we believe to be important, significant, and valuable. Therefore, if we profess with our mouths that God's Word holds a place of high value and significance in our lives, then we should give valuable and significant time to studying it. You have more free-time in the day than you might think. It's just a matter of how you prioritize your time.

Someone once said, "The Devil is not afraid of the Bible that has dust on it."[66] Satan hates the Bible. He fears the Word of God because he knows the great power it contains. He also knows that the Word is one of the primary sources for the Christian's growth and strength, and that the greater a Christian knows and obeys the Bible, the greater of a threat he/she is to the kingdom of darkness (Eph 6:17). Is it any wonder, then, that Satan tries so hard—and is so successful—in distracting people from studying the Bible? He's often effective is deceiving people with the lies that the Bible is boring, that it's too hard to understand, or that there's more fun or important things to do than digging into God's Word.

Hebrews 4:12 says that "the word of God *is* living and powerful, and sharper than any two-edged sword, piercing even to the division of soul and spirit, and of joints and marrow, and is a discerner of the thoughts and intents of the heart." A surgeon's scalpel is an incredibly sharp tool that cuts through flesh and all parts of the human body, but it does so for the purpose of exposing where disease and life-threatening dangers exist and to cut out those things in order to protect life. God's Word does the same thing, spiritually speaking. It's like a sharp sword that pierces into people's souls, convicting them as it exposes their sin and reveals that they need to change their lifestyles and their way of thinking. It can be a painful and uncomfortable experience, but it's necessary, and the truth often hurts. No wonder, then, that so many people choose not to

---

[66] Anonymous as quoted in Frank S. Mead, ed., *12,000 Religious Quotations* (1965; repr., Grand Rapids, MI: Baker Book House, 1989), 23.

read the Bible! They don't want to be confronted with the fact that they need to change; they don't want to feel convicted; they don't want to change or be held accountable. Therefore, they avoid a serious study of God's Word.

Boredom

Second, maybe your attitude is that the Bible is just so *boring* to read and hard to understand. (I can't count how many times I've heard this as a youth pastor and as a teacher in Christian schools.) Now, if you find the Bible boring and hard to understand, permit me to suggest something to you: one of the reasons you think the Bible doesn't make sense and is, therefore, boring might be because you don't know how to study it. This is in no way an insult on your intelligence.

Like with most things in life, if you want to understand a certain concept or book, there are specific methods and rules you must follow in order to guide yourself to the most accurate interpretation and conclusion. Algebra is not that difficult to understand (and that's saying a lot because I'm not the best at math); it's just about following rules and methods. If you understand the rules and follow them, piece of cake. You may still make a mistake here and there and end up with a wrong conclusion, but you're much more likely to comprehend the problem if you know and follow the rules and methods. If you *don't* understand the rules, however, then you'll probably hate math, and understandably so. The same concept applies to the Bible. When reading the Bible, if you don't know the right methods to employ in order to study and interpret it accurately, then you can very easily become frustrated and find it to be a boring book that makes no sense. Therefore, if you want some great tools for how to study the Bible correctly and, as a result, discover a treasure hoard of riches when you dig into the Word, see Appendix B.

Another reason people oftentimes find the Bible to be a boring book has to do with the attitude of the heart. If your heart and mind are not right toward God and His Word when you come to read it, then this wrong attitude can—and usually does—negatively impact your view toward the Word. Consider this: when was the last time you approached the Bible and opened it with the genuine belief that what you were about to read is the very living, active, powerful Word of the eternal Creator of the universe, who has revealed to you what He is like and who actually wants to speak to you and help you and radically change your life as you study that Book? Do you think that if we came to the Bible with *that* perspective each time we read it, our lives would be a bit different? Absolutely!

Willful Disobedience

A third way that we can minimize the significance of God's Word in our lives is by willfully choosing to break its commands.

> **Scenario #1**: You choose to tell a lie to get yourself out of a jam. You know that lying is sinful and that God commands you in His Word not to do it, yet you think that it's not *that big of an issue* in this case.

Clearly, your attitude is that obeying God's Word isn't *that significant* right now in this situation.

> **Scenario #2**: You're angry at someone who is in authority over you. You deliberately choose to disrespect them and rebel. You know that God's Word says to honor those in authority over you but, in your mind, you either think that it's perfectly okay to disrespect them or you know that it's wrong but you simply don't care.

The point in these two examples is that your actions clearly don't reflect an attitude of reverence for God's Word. Rather, they reveal an attitude that says that God's Word isn't significant enough for you to obey, at least not in that instance. When we have a flippant attitude toward God's Word and willfully disregard His commands, we're despising the Word, not esteeming it.

A few other very subtle ways we can despise God's Word are to read it often but (1) have a complacent, routine-like attitude where we fail to pay much attention to what we're reading, (2) have a bitter and resentful attitude toward God and His Word because either we don't like His commands or we feel like God hasn't come through on His promises to us or, well, fill in the blank, and/or (3) think that reading is enough and nothing more is needed, i.e., we fail to obey what it says and are, therefore, hearers and not doers of the Word.

A Case Study: The Ancient Israelites

The ancient Israelites experienced terrible destruction at the hands of the Assyrians and Babylonians. This destruction consisted of starvation, slaughter, and, among other things, captivity into foreign lands. You may wonder what the reason was for such miserable destruction. The Old Testament prophet Amos, along with many other prophets, reveals that Israel's catastrophic destruction was part of God's judgment that He brought upon the Israelites. What merited such punishment? In Amos 2:4, God says that it was "because they have despised the law of the Lord." Interesting! Maybe if the Israelites had read Proverbs 13:13 (maybe they had but just willfully ignored it), they would have taken heed to the warning from their wisest ancestor. But let's go a little deeper. There's more to Amos 2:4.

Immediately after saying that the Israelites despised God's Word, Amos then says that they "have not kept His commandments."

This might seem like a pretty obvious result of the previous statement. If someone despises God's Word, then it naturally follows that he/she won't obey what is written and commanded therein. But notice the cause and effect that is taking place here, and the consequences that follow from despising the Word.

First, despising the Word will result in a failure to obey the Word. Second, despising God's Word will result in believing lies. In the next part of verse four, Amos says, "Their lies lead them astray." If you despise God's Word of *truth*, then naturally you'll believe lies and be led astray by them. Remember, truth keeps you on the right path, whereas lies lead you down a road to destruction.

Third, despising the Word will cause you to forget history and/or to fail to learn from it. After saying that their lies led the Israelites astray, Amos then gets specific: "lies after which their fathers walked." Interesting! Oftentimes one of the effects of despising God's Word is a failure to (1) learn from history, namely, from the mistakes of those who have gone before you, and (2) avoid making those same mistakes in your own life.

Fourth, the ultimate effect—or consequence—of despising the Word is to experience God's judgment. In the case of the Israelites, God declares, "But I will send a fire upon Judah, and it shall devour the palaces of Jerusalem" (v. 5). And guess what: this exact judgment happened when King Nebuchadnezzar of Babylon sacked Jerusalem three different times. Much can be learned from ancient Israel. The ultimate consequence of sowing a seed of despising God's Word of truth is to reap destruction.

The prophet Isaiah tells us something similar about the ancient Israelites. He declares that fierce judgment and destruction were going to come upon the Israelites "because they have rejected the law of the LORD of hosts, and despised the word of the Holy One of Israel" (Isa 5:24). This is exactly what Solomon forewarned hundreds of years prior, and true to form, God's Word was fulfilled and ancient Israel was destroyed.[67]

Attitude Says It All

Our attitude says everything. What kind of message do you think we're sending to God when we have the attitude that our time is too valuable to sit down and take 30 minutes or an hour to really study and meditate upon His Word; that we're too busy with other things to read what He has chosen to reveal to us in His written Word; that other things in our lives are more enjoyable than delving into the Word and discovering what God has revealed about Himself and His amazing plans for our lives? This type of attitude sends a message loud and clear, namely that the Bible isn't *that* significant, *that* important, *that* necessary to study often. In essence, we're saying that studying God's Word isn't very high on our priority list, and that its role in our lives isn't all that significant—i.e., that we can get by just fine in the Christian life without the Word. Imagine how God feels when we express such an attitude toward His love letter to us.

So, do you want to ruin your life? If your answer is *yes*, then you should thank Solomon because he has given you a simple prescription for disaster: just despise the Word of God. Do this, and you're sure to meet with destruction.

---

[67] See also Isaiah 30:1-14 (key verse: 12) in which God proclaims judgment upon Israel for their rejection of Him, and because they despised His Word.

12

THE LIFE-SAVING ALTERNATIVE: REVERE THE WORD

If you have even a shred of godly wisdom in you, then you're probably thinking right about now, "I don't want to destroy my life." Well, thanks be to God that there's hope. So far, we've looked at only half of what Proverbs 13:13 says, "He who despises the word will be destroyed." Let's now examine the rest of the verse: "but he who fears the commandment will be rewarded." First of all, the idea behind the word *fear* that is used here isn't that you're constantly afraid of the Bible. Rather, the Hebrew word used here also means *reverence*. According to the dictionary, *revere* means, "To regard with awe, great respect, or devotion." The dictionary further says that this term implies "the deepest respect and esteem for a person, an object, or a deity. *Revere* has a sense of treasuring with profound respect."

To revere God's Word is the polar opposite of despising it. To give you an idea of what reverence for God's Word looks like, let's examine a few more quotes from some of America's Founding Fathers. Benjamin Rush, signer of the *Declaration of Independence*, a surgeon general in the Continental Army, and known as the father of American medicine, wrote, "The only means of establishing and perpetuating our republican forms of government is the universal education of our youth in the principles of Christianity by means of

189

the Bible."[68] Wow, what an incredible view of Scripture, and with such profound implications! But that's not all. Rush also said, "The Bible, when not read in schools, is seldom read in any subsequent period of life…. [The Bible] should be read in our schools in preference to all other books."[69] Yet again, Rush proclaims, "The great enemy of the salvation of man, in my opinion, never invented a more effective means of limiting Christianity from the world than by persuading mankind that it was improper to read the Bible at schools."[70] It's quite evident that Benjamin Rush possessed a holy reverence for the Word of God.

To revere the Bible means to hold it in high esteem, to cherish it, to regard it with great devotion. But such an attitude implies that you're an avid student of the Word and that you live in obedience to what it says. In short, to revere the Word is to read and heed what it says. The life-saving alternative to destruction is to possess this kind of reverence for the Word of God.

Maybe you're wondering, "Okay, I don't currently have such a reverence for God's Word, but I want it. How do I get it?" There can be several steps to take, but let me mention just two. First, ask for it. Since God wants you to have such a reverence for His Word, then it's pleasing to Him when you ask Him to work and instill such a reverence into your heart. A lot of times we don't have something because we simply don't ask God for it (Jas 4:2). So, ask God for help. Also, you can't go wrong when praying Scripture into your life. Therefore, a good prayer to offer to God on this issue is Ephesians 1:18 (NASB), wherein Paul says, "*I pray that* the eyes of your heart may be enlightened." Ask God to do this very thing to you.

---

[68] Benjamin Rush, *Essays, Literary, Moral & Philosophical*, 2nd ed. (Philadelphia, PA: Thomas & William Bradford, 1806), 112.

[69] Ibid., 94, 100.

[70] Ibid., *Letters of Benjamin Rush*, vol. 1, ed. L. H. Butterfield (Princeton, NJ: Princeton University Press, 1951), 521.

A second way to obtain a greater reverence for the Word is to start reading and studying it more. Oftentimes a person will gain a greater love and admiration for the Bible the more he/she spends time delving deep into its pages of rich truth. And keep in mind that as you read it, you aren't just reading any old book. You're reading the very words of God Himself, and He wants to work in your heart and change your life as you study His Word. John Quincy Adams, the son of John Adams and the sixth president of the United States, said:

> So great is my veneration for the Bible & so strong my belief that when duly read & meditated upon, it is of all the books in the world, that which contributes most to make men good, wise, & happy, that the earlier my children begin to read it & the more steadily they pursue the practice of reading it throughout their lives, the more lively & confident will be my hopes that they will prove useful citizens to their Country respectable members of society & a real blessing to their Parents.[71]

Proverbs 13:13 says that the person who possesses such reverence for God's Word "will be rewarded." *Rewarded with what?* you may ask. Recall the previous list in this chapter of some of the things that God's Word accomplishes, and then consider the blessings that come from cherishing this beloved Book. The person who loves, reveres, and obeys God's Word will experience the following: life, sound teaching, needful rebuke and correction that leads to growth, instruction in the ways of righteousness, growth in maturity, healing, strength and edification, spiritual freedom, comfort, revival, support to hold him/her up, sanctification, spiritual cleansing and protection, discernment and direction, great peace, stability,

---

[71] John Quincy Adams, "From John Quincy Adams George Washington Adams, 1 September 1811," National Archives: Founders Online, accessed November 17, 2020, https://founders.archives.gov/documents/Adams/99-03-02-2021.

understanding, wisdom, deliverance, and so much more.

Do you want these good things for your life, or would you rather have their alternatives and meet with destruction? If the former, then choose to do as Solomon says in Proverbs 13:13 and fear—or revere—the Word of God.

Not only does Solomon promise rich reward to those who revere the Word of God, but so does Jesus Himself. In Luke 11:28, Jesus says, "Blessed *are* those who hear the word of God and keep it." If you read the context of this verse, you will see that Jesus said that the person who hears and obeys God's Word is even more blessed than Jesus' own mother, Mary, who had the blessed privilege of carrying the Savior of the world in her womb and then raising Him. That's incredible! It's hard to imagine a greater blessing than *that*. Yet, Jesus said that whoever hears and fears—obeys—His Word is even more blessed than Mary. Clearly, Jesus must have placed a lot of value on obedience to His Word.

There is an interesting parallel between Solomon's words in Proverbs 13:13 and the words of his father, King David. In Psalm 1:1-2, David says, "Blessed *is* the man who walks not in the counsel of the ungodly, nor stands in the path of sinners, nor sits in the seat of the scornful; but his delight *is* in the law of the LORD, and in His law he meditates day and night." David tells us that the person is blessed whose attitude toward God's Word is one of delight, adoration, and reverence. This kind of person can't get enough of the Word; he/she meditates on it all the time. Is this descriptive of your own personal attitude toward God's Word?

What else does David tell us about this blessed person? In verse three he says that the result of having such a reverence for God's Word is that "He shall be like a tree planted by the rivers of water, that brings forth its fruit in its season, whose leaf also shall not wither; and whatever he does shall prosper." Let me expound on just how profound this picture is that David paints.

I love hiking and exploring. In San Diego, the landscape is pretty brown for at least half of the year because it's generally a hot, dry climate. Every time I've gone hiking during the summer months, I can always tell when there is a river or stream in the distance because there is a trail of trees that are green and thriving with life. Everything around them may be brown, dried up, and dead, but the trees will be lush. Why? Because they're "planted by the rivers of water" and, as a result, their leaves don't wither but are full of life because they're constantly receiving the good nutrients and water that they need. Can you see the spiritual application? The person who loves God's Word and meditates on it daily will be a spiritually mature Christian who is constantly growing, thriving, and leading a biblically prosperous life.

Solomon also promises in Proverbs 19:16 that "he who keeps the commandment keeps his soul." In other words, by living in obedience to God's Word, a person is protecting his/her own soul. Satan desires the souls of men. He can't have the soul of a Christian because it has been bought and paid for by the blood of Jesus. The next best thing that Satan can attempt is to damage and ruin the Christian's soul by distracting and pulling it away from Christ, and you can bet that he's working nonstop to make that happen. How can the Christian guard his/her soul? Obey the Word of God. There are countless things that are competing for the attention and dominance of your soul. Thankfully, if you belong to Jesus, you're safe and secure in His mighty, everlasting arms. However, this doesn't mean that you have no responsibilities. You need to avidly seek to know the Lord more and to obey His Word. So, do you want to experience the blessings rather than the destruction? If *yes*, then hear and fear the Word. Read it and heed it. Do this, and God promises many times over that you will be blessed many times over.

A Final Thought

I will close this chapter with a few questions as food-for-thought. Should we live in accordance with what the Bible teaches? If we believe that the Bible is truly God's Word and that it gives us divine revelation and instruction for how to live and to glorify God, then it's obvious that we need to conform our lives to its precepts and obey its commands. But how can we live by and obey God's Word if we don't know what it says? And how can we know what it says unless we eagerly and diligently study it? Therefore, dear reader, do as David did and hide God's Word in your heart.

13

AT THE CROSSROADS

In this book, we have examined just six of the many ways in which you can destroy your life. We have also seen the antidotes to these destructive sins. God has set before you a choice. In the words of Moses, God has "set before you life and death, blessing and cursing" (Deut 30:19). You can choose to destroy your life by walking in any of these six sins, or you can choose to protect yourself from destruction and to abide in the blessing of God by walking in obedience to His Word. And so, my question to you is this: what do you want for your life? Do you want destruction and death, or life and the blessing of God? The choice is yours. And my exhortation to you echoes that of Moses once again: "choose life" (Deut 30:19).

In closing out this book, I want to encourage you, dear reader, to fix your eyes on Christ. As you reach the end of this book, it's possible that you might feel pretty hopeless, burdened by the weight of your failures to overcome sin in your past, and thinking the future will be no better. Or, maybe you feel quite the opposite: you're refreshed, encouraged, rejuvenated, and you have a passion to fight against the flesh and to walk in holiness and in victory over sin.

Regardless of which of the two ends of the spectrum you may land on currently, I encourage you to do this one thing: be totally dependent upon the Spirit to help you live for Christ. Don't be disheartened and think that you have sinned and failed too much to the point that there's no hope of honoring the Lord with your life. He knows we are weak and that we are just dust. He is wonderfully patient and gracious in all our failures. There is restoration and healing where there is true, biblical repentance. We all fall so utterly short, and the grace of God is marvelously great toward those who humble themselves before Him.

On the other hand, guard yourself from self-righteousness and pride. Don't attempt to conquer sin and walk in holiness in your own strength, because it will never work. Beware of becoming wise in your own eyes. Don't get caught in the trap of believing you can honor God in the flesh. We so desperately need the grace of God and the help of the Holy Spirit to live a life that is well-pleasing to the Lord. Jesus told His disciples that "without Me you can do nothing" (John 15:5b). Therefore, live with the constant recognition of your need for the Lord's grace, and choose to follow the leading of the Spirit.

It is wonderful news to know that God has provided us with all we need to live Christ-honoring lives. He has given us His Spirit, His divine power (2 Pet. 1:2-3; Eph. 3:20), and the whole armor of God. Therefore, be encouraged that it's not all dependent on you to grow in sanctification. The Holy Spirit will strengthen, guide, and help you as you yield to Him. "…The Spirit of truth… will guide you into all truth" (John 16:13).

Dear reader, "Trust in the Lord forever, for in YAH, the Lord, is everlasting strength" (Isa. 26:4).

Appendix A:

A Personal Relationship with God

What is a personal relationship with Jesus Christ? To begin with, there's great news. The God of the Bible is a *personal* God. What does that mean? It means that God cares about His creatures, human beings, and He wants to have personal relationships with them. In fact, He created them for this very purpose: to glorify Him and to enjoy a beautiful, personal relationship with Him forever. This *personal* characteristic of God is evident throughout the Bible.

This is quite different from the gods of many other world religions. These gods are often impersonal, they don't care about humans, their well-being, their pain and suffering, or about having a relationship with them. Thankfully, the God of the Bible is the only true and living God.[72]

Mankind started out with a perfect relationship with God in the Garden of Eden. Unfortunately, that relationship was severed and tarnished when mankind sinned against God by disobeying His perfect command (see Genesis 2 and 3). Sin, also defined as lawlessness (1 John 3:4), is disobedience to God. Sin ruins relationship, and every person is a sinner. The apostle Paul tells us in Romans 3:23 that "all have sinned and fall short of the glory of God." And there are consequences for sin. Romans 6:23a tells us that "the

---

[72] If you have doubts about whether this is true or whether God even exists at all, see the following helpful resources: alwaysbeready.com. See also, crossexamined.org. See also, Norman Geisler, *Christian Apologetics* 2nd ed. ().

wages of sin *is* death." In other words, sin comes at a price and that price is death—not just physical death at the end of this life on earth, but spiritual death as well.

What is spiritual death? Well, think about it like this: spiritual life is knowing God (John 17:3), i.e., having a personal relationship with Him. Therefore, spiritual death is a severed relationship with God, i.e., a life of separation from Him. The consequences of separation from God are far-reaching (e.g., living in spiritual darkness, being blinded from God's truth, having no hope in this world, to name just a few).

Now, some people would say, "Well, I'm not *that bad* of a sinner," to which I would reply, *According to whose standard?* Are you a pretty *good* sinner (I'm not using *good* here in the sense of being good *at sinning* but rather being a good person who is a sinner)? If you say *yes*, then by whose standard are you coming to such a conclusion: the standard of your *own* measurement of goodness, or by *God's* standard of goodness? Oftentimes when comparing ourselves with other people, we don't look all that bad. But there's a fatal flaw with using this standard for measuring goodness, namely, that this isn't *God's* standard for goodness. God's standard for goodness doesn't say, "Hey, as long as you turn out to be better than other people when you compare yourself to them, then you qualify as *good enough* to get to Heaven." Comparing ourselves with other people is the wrong standard by which we should judge whether or not we're good. Therefore, you may be asking, "Then what *is* the standard?" I'm glad you asked.

Let's look back at Romans 3:23. It says that "all have sinned and fall short of the glory of God." The *New Living Translation* renders this verse, "For everyone has sinned; we all fall short of God's glorious standard." The standard for whether you are good is whether you measure up to the glory of God. Yikes! That sounds quite impossible. How can one successfully measure up to God's glory? Well, to start, you'd have to be completely sinless which, as we've already established, no human is. But just in case any readers want to say they've never sinned, let me quote the apostle John: "If we say that we have no sin, we deceive ourselves, and the truth is not in us.... If we say that we have not sinned, we make Him a liar, and His word is not in us" (1 John 1:8, 10).

So, what is "God's glorious standard" for people? Jesus tells us that all of God's commandments in Scripture are summed up in just two commands, the greatest of all commandments: "'You shall love the LORD your God with all your heart, with all your soul, and with all your mind.' This is the first and great commandment. And the second is like it: 'You shall love your neighbor as yourself'" (Matt 22:37-39). Regarding the first command, Mark 12:30 adds loving God "with all of your strength." If you're the person who says, "I'm not *that bad* of a sinner," let's measure you up to God's glorious standard of these two commandments.

Ask yourself: do you always—and have you always in your entire life—perfectly love God with every bit of your heart, with every part of your soul, with the entirety of your mind, and with every ounce of your strength, without fail? If you—and every other human being, for that matter—are going to be honest, your answer is a resounding and emphatic *no*. In fact, if we did the math, we'd find that we have failed much more often than we have succeeded at obeying this command. Therefore, you have already fallen so far and terribly short of "God's glorious standard." But that's not all; there's another commandment to consider.

Have you always perfectly loved your fellow human beings in the way that God commands in His Word? Again, if we're all going to be honest, we'll admit that we have fallen short and have failed more often than we've succeeded, at least by God's standard. So, we have totally missed the mark and fallen short of God's glorious standard. Therefore, there are many serious consequences to these sins of ours, one of the most important being a severed relationship with God and eternal separation from Him both in this life on earth and in Hell in the afterlife. Remember, the price of sin is death. Let these words and the reality of these devastating consequences sink in.

At this point you may be feeling pretty hopeless and wondering if there is any good news. Thankfully, there is. The word *gospel* actually means that very thing: *good news*. What is the Gospel? It is the good news that Jesus Christ has provided a way for people to be reconciled back to God. *Reconcile* means to make peace between two parties. In this case, it is peace between us and God. What shattered that peace in the past? Sin. And because we're sinners full of sin, we could never do enough good works to renew peace between us and God. The only way for peace and right relationship with God to be restored is by our sins being washed away. Our good works cannot wash away or cancel out our sin. Therefore, Jesus did *for* you what no one else could: He voluntarily laid down His perfect life as a substitute in your place to bear the punishment for your sins. He died on a cross and His blood was shed so that you could be saved from sin and eternal separation from God in Hell. Here are a few passages that explain this:

- "For God so loved the world that He gave His only begotten Son, that whoever believes in Him should not perish but have everlasting life" (John 3:16).
- "But God demonstrates His own love toward us, in that while we were still sinners, Christ died for us" (Rom 5:8).
- "For I delivered to you first of all that which I also received: that Christ died for our sins according to the Scriptures, and that He was buried, and that He rose again the third day according to the Scriptures" (1 Cor 15:3-4).

Jesus died in our place; He took our punishment for us. He died but then rose from the dead, proving that His claims are true and that whoever places their trust in Him will be saved. We are promised that "if you confess with your mouth the Lord Jesus and believe in your heart that God has raised Him from the dead, you will be saved…. For 'whoever calls on the name of the LORD shall be saved'" (Rom 10:9, 13). Jesus is the only One who can save you. There is no other way. As He Himself said, "I am the way, the truth, and the life. No one comes to the Father except through Me" (John 14:6). It is not only believing these things *about* Jesus that you need to do, though this is necessary. There are plenty of people who believe true things *about* Jesus, but they aren't saved. Belief *about* Jesus is essential, but it alone is not enough. It's also about believing *in* Him, i.e., placing your trust in Him to save you.

So how does a person begin a personal relationship with God? Well, begin by acknowledging the biblical truths mentioned above about your sin and then repent (i.e., change your mind/attitude) of your sin and place your trust in Jesus alone. According to the passages mentioned above, when a person does this, God gives him/her eternal life. What is eternal life? Jesus defined it for us, "And this is eternal life, that they may know You, the only true God, and Jesus Christ whom You have sent" (John 17:3). Eternal life is a renewal of that personal relationship with God that was broken at the Fall in the Garden of Eden. And this eternal life doesn't begin in Heaven; it begins the moment a person places his/her trust in Jesus.

So, you know what it means to have a personal relationship with God. What now? Well, if you've never done what is mentioned above about confessing your sinfulness, repenting of that sin, and then placing your faith in Jesus Christ to save you, then I urge you to do that, and to do it now. Paul tells us that "now is the day of salvation" (2 Cor 6:2). Therefore, don't put it off. Rather, turn to Jesus *today* and be saved. Surrender your life to Him, commit your life to following Jesus, and live your life for the glory of God by the help and power of the Holy Spirit.

Appendix B:

Studying the Bible

It was that great Founding Father of America, Elias Boudinot, who so rightly said that "it is for want [lack] of understanding the scriptures... that so little value is set upon them by the world at large."[73]

One of the oft-occurring problems with many Christians is that, when reading the Bible, they want to read it through a 21st century, Western lens. But the Bible isn't a Western book. It's a Jewish Book, written thousands of years ago in a different part of the world and in different cultural and historical settings than our own. Therefore, we must study the Bible in those contexts. Otherwise, we are sure to (1) come away with some terrible misinterpretations and misapplications of the Word, and/or (2) find the Bible difficult and even boring to read. The better the we understand the context of a given passage or book we're studying, the more it will make sense, and the better, more accurate interpretations and applications we can make.

Another subtle trap that many Christians often fall into is reading the Bible just to try to find some immediate application for their lives. Now, to be sure, there is plenty in the Bible that we can apply to our lives even thousands of years after it was written (that's one of the beautiful things about God's Word, it transcends time), but the problem is that we sometimes read it for only one purpose: to see what we can get out of it. In other words, we want to have a

---

[73] Elias Boudinot, *The Age of Revelation, or the Age of Reason Shewn to be An Age of Infidelity* (Philadelphia, PA: Asbury Dickins, 1801), xv-xvi.

really cool, spiritual, emotional experience when reading the Bible. This is often a selfish motive for studying Scripture. In other words, our motive for reading has become more focused on ourselves and is self-centered rather than the focus being on glorifying and honoring God. And the problem is that when we don't have that amazing experience, we can become discouraged, bored, or even bitter toward God for not making it more "exciting" of an experience.

But the Bible doesn't exist simply for you to have a cool experience or to feel something spiritual when you read it. Rather, one of its purposes it to help you grow, and growing doesn't always entail you experiencing warm, fuzzy, "spiritual" feelings. Sometimes you may have amazing eye-opening experiences, and that's great. But other times you may not, and that is not necessarily a bad thing. This could, at times, be a test from God to see whether we're going to keep faithfully studying His Word even when you don't have a seemingly profound experience or when you don't feel like it. Faithfulness is key.

As I mentioned in chapter seven, a possible—and probable—reason many Christians find the Bible to be a boring, hard-to-understand Book is because they don't know how to study it properly. There are certain guidelines you must follow when studying Scripture in order to ensure the best possible interpretation and application of it. Therefore, I will provide a few very helpful resources here that will serve as guides and instruction manuals to you in how to correctly study the Bible. Visit this link for a very helpful breakdown of the Inductive Bible Study method: https://biblestudy.tips/inductive-bible-study/.[74] A couple of very helpful books include Roy B. Zuck's *Basic Bible Interpretation: A Practical Guide to Discovering Biblical Truth*[75] and Cory M. Marsh's *A Primer*

---

[74] BibleStudy.Tips, "Inductive Bible Study: A Step-by-Step Guide," accessed April 17, 2023, https://biblestudy.tips/inductive-bible-study/.

[75] Roy B. Zuck, *Basic Bible Interpretation: A Practical Guide to Discovering Biblical Truth* (Colorado Springs, CO: Victor, 1991).

on Biblical Literacy.[76] No matter your level of education, you will find these books very helpful in your endeavor to understand, interpret, and apply the Word of God correctly.

---

[76] Cory M. Marsh, *A Primer on Biblical Literacy* (El Cajon, CA: Southern California Seminary Press, 2022).

Appendix C:

Proverbs on the Tongue

Proverbs:

10:11 – "The mouth of the righteous *is* a well of life, but violence covers the mouth of the wicked."

10:18 – "Whoever hides hatred *has* lying lips, and whoever spreads slander *is* a fool."

10:19 – "In the multitude of words sin is not lacking, but he who restrains his lips *is* wise."

10:20 – "The tongue of the righteous *is* choice silver; the heart of the wicked *is worth* little."

10:21 – "The lips of the righteous feed many, but fools die for lack of wisdom."

10:31 – "The mouth of the righteous brings forth wisdom, but the perverse tongue will be cut out."

10:32 – "The lips of the righteous know what is acceptable, but the mouth of the wicked *what is* perverse."

11:9 – "The hypocrite with *his* mouth destroys his neighbor, but through knowledge the righteous will be delivered."

11:11 – "By the blessing of the upright the city is exalted, but it is overthrown by the mouth of the wicked."

11:12 – "The one who denounces his neighbor lacks wisdom, but the one who has discernment keeps silent." (NET)

11:13 – "A gossip betrays a confidence, but a trustworthy person keeps a secret." (NIV)

12:6 – "The words of the wicked *are,* "Lie in wait for blood," but the mouth of the upright will deliver them."

12:19 – "The truthful lip shall be established forever, but a lying tongue *is* but for a moment."

12:22 – "Lying lips *are* an abomination to the LORD, but those who deal truthfully *are* His delight."

13:3 – "He who guards his mouth preserves his life, *but* he who opens wide his lips shall have destruction."

14:3 – "In the mouth of a fool *is* a rod of pride, but the lips of the wise will preserve them."

15:1 – "A soft answer turns away wrath, but a harsh word stirs up anger."

15:2 – "The tongue of the wise uses knowledge rightly, but the mouth of fools pours forth foolishness."

15:4 – "A wholesome tongue *is* a tree of life, but perverseness in it breaks the spirit."

15:7 – "The lips of the wise disperse knowledge, but the heart of the fool *does* not *do* so."

15:14 – "The heart of him who has understanding seeks knowledge, but the mouth of fools feeds on foolishness."

15:23 – "A man has joy by the answer of his mouth, and a word *spoken* in due season, how good *it is!*"

15:28 – "The heart of the righteous studies how to answer, but the mouth of the wicked pours forth evil."

16:1 – "The preparations of the heart *belong* to man, but the answer of the tongue *is* from the LORD."

16:13 – "Righteous lips *are* the delight of kings, and they love him who speaks *what is* right."

16:23 – "The heart of the wise teaches his mouth, and adds learning to his lips."

16:24 – "Pleasant words *are like* a honeycomb, sweetness to the soul and health to the bones."

16:27 – "An ungodly man digs up evil, and *it is* on his lips like a burning fire."

16:28 – "A perverse man sows strife, and a whisperer separates the best of friends."

17:4 – "An evildoer gives heed to false lips; a liar listens eagerly to a spiteful tongue."

17:7 – "Excellent speech is not becoming to a fool, much less lying lips to a prince."

17:9 – "He who covers a transgression seeks love, but he who repeats a matter separates friends."

17:20 – "He who has a deceitful heart finds no good, and he who has a perverse tongue falls into evil."

17:27 – "He who has knowledge spares his words, *and* a man of understanding is of a calm spirit."

17:28 – "Even a fool is counted wise when he holds his peace; *when* he shuts his lips, *he is considered* perceptive."

18:2 – "A fool has no delight in understanding, but in expressing his own heart."

18:4 – "The words of a man's mouth *are* deep waters; the wellspring of wisdom *is* a flowing brook."

18:6 – "A fool's lips enter into contention, and his mouth calls for blows."

18:7 – "A fool's mouth *is* his destruction, and his lips *are* the snare of his soul."

18:8 – "The words of a talebearer *are* like tasty trifles, and they go down into the inmost body."

18:13 – "He who answers a matter before he hears *it,* it *is* folly and shame to him."

18:20 – "A man's stomach shall be satisfied from the fruit of his mouth; *from* the produce of his lips he shall be filled."

18:21 – "Death and life *are* in the power of the tongue, and those who love it will eat its fruit."

19:1 – "Better *is* the poor who walks in his integrity than *one who is* perverse in his lips, and is a fool."

19:5 – "A false witness will not go unpunished, and *he who* speaks lies will not escape."

19:28 – "A disreputable witness scorns justice, and the mouth of the wicked devours iniquity."

20:15 – "There is gold and a multitude of rubies, but the lips of knowledge *are* a precious jewel."

20:19 – "He who goes about *as* a talebearer reveals secrets; therefore do not associate with one who flatters with his lips."

21:6 – "Getting treasures by a lying tongue *is* the fleeting fantasy of those who seek death."

21:23 – "Whoever guards his mouth and tongue keeps his soul from troubles."

21:28 – A false witness shall perish, but the man who hears *him* will speak endlessly."

23:9 – "Do not speak in the hearing of a fool, for he will despise the wisdom of your words."

24:1-2 – "Do not be envious of evil men, nor desire to be with them; for their heart devises violence, and their lips talk of troublemaking."

24:26 – "He who gives a right answer kisses the lips."

24:28 – "Do not be a witness against your neighbor without cause, for would you deceive with your lips?"

25:11 – "A word fitly spoken *is like* apples of gold in settings of silver."

25:15 – "By long forbearance a ruler is persuaded, and a gentle tongue breaks a bone."

25:23 – "The north wind brings forth rain, and a backbiting tongue an angry countenance."

26:2 – "Like a flitting sparrow, like a flying swallow, so a curse without cause shall not alight."

26:7 – "*Like* the legs of the lame that hang limp *is* a proverb in the mouth of fools."

26:9 – "*Like* a thorn *that* goes into the hand of a drunkard *is* a proverb in the mouth of fools."

26:20 – "Where *there is* no wood, the fire goes out; and where *there is* no talebearer, strife ceases."

26:22 – "The words of a talebearer *are* as wounds, and they go down into the innermost parts of the belly." (KJV)

26:23 – "Fervent lips with a wicked heart *are like* earthenware covered with silver dross."

26:24-26 – "He who hates, disguises *it* with his lips, and lays up deceit within himself; when he speaks kindly, do not believe him, for *there are* seven abominations in his heart; *though his* hatred is covered by deceit, his wickedness will be revealed before the assembly."

29:20 – "Do you see a man hasty in his words? *There is* more hope for a fool than for him."

30:11-12 – "*There is* a generation *that* curses its father, and does not bless its mother. *There is* a generation *that is* pure in its own eyes, *yet* is not washed from its filthiness."

31:26 – Said of the virtuous woman, "She opens her mouth with wisdom, and on her tongue *is* the law of kindness."

Bibliography

Adams, John. *"The Works of John Adams, vol. 10 (Letters 1811-1825, Indexes)* [1854]."* Online Library of Liberty. Accessed November 17, 2020. https://oll.libertyfund.org/titles/adams-the-works-of-john-adams-vol-10-letters-1811-1825-indexes.

Adams, John Quincy. "From John Quincy Adams George Washington Adams, 1 September 1811." National Archives: Founders Online. Accessed November 17, 2020. https://founders.archives.gov/documents/Adams/99-03-02-2021.

Anonymous as quoted in Mead, Frank S., ed. *12,000 Religious Quotations.* 1965; Reprint, Grand Rapids, MI: Baker Book House, 1989.

Saint Augustine. *The Soliloquies of St. Augustine.* Translated by Rose Elizabeth Cleveland. Boston, MA: Little, Brown, and Company, 1910.

Blaszczynski, Alexander. "Excessive Pornography Use: Empirically-Enhanced Treatment Interventions." *Australian Clinical Psychologist* 2, no. 1 (2016): 1-7.

Boudinot, Elias. *The Age of Revelation, or the Age of Reason Shewn to be An Age of Infidelity.* Philadelphia, PA: Asbury Dickins, 1801.

Brande, Lauren. "Women with Porn Addictions." American Addiction Centers. August 23, 2020. Accessed November 11, 2020. https://www.projectknow.com/porn-addiction/women/.

Covenant Eyes. "Pornography Statistics." CovenantEyes.com. Accessed November 10, 2020. https://www.covenanteyes.com/pornstats/.

Dawkins, Richard. *The God Delusion*. New York, NY: Mariner Books, 2008.

Benjamin Franklin as quoted in Unknown Author. *Liber Facetiarum: Being a Collection of Curious and Interesting Anecdotes*. Newcastle Upon Tyne, England: Printed by and for D. Akenhead and Sons, 1809.

G., Katie. "100+ Personal Stories Of Harm Or Negative Effects by Pornography, Prostitution, Stripping, Sexual Slavery, Sex Trafficking, Sexual Harassment, Sexual Abuse, Our Pornified Society, etc." AntiPornography.org. Accessed August 6, 2020. https://www.antipornography.org/harm_stories.html#17 1863.

Geisler, Norman. *Christian Apologetics*. 2nd ed. Grand Rapids, MI: Baker Academic, 2013.

Geisler, Norman L., and William E. Nix. *A General Introduction To The Bible*. Chicago, IL: Moody Press, 1986.

Harris, Sam. "Sam Harris: On Interpreting Scripture." Youtube.com. Accessed June 23, 2020. https://www.youtube.com/watch?v=8zV3vIXZ-1Y.

———. "The God Debate II: Harris vs. Craig." Youtube.com. April 12, 2011. Accessed June 23, 2020. https://www.youtube.com/watch?v=yqaHXKLRKzg.

Hewitt, James S. ed. *Illustrations Unlimited*. Wheaton, IL: Tyndale House Publishers, 1988.

Hughes, R. Kent. *Disciplines of a Godly Man*. Rev. ed. Wheaton, IL: Crossway Books, 2001.

Jay, John. *John Jay: The Winning of the Peace. Unpublished Papers 1780-1784*. Edited by Richard B. Morris, New York, NY: Harper & Row Publishers, 1980.

MacDonald, William. *Believer's Bible Commentary*. Nashville, TN: Thomas Nelson Publishers, 1995.

Niemoller, Martin. "Martin Niemoller: 'First They Came For the Socialists….'" Holocaust Encyclopedia. March 30, 2012. Accessed April 13, 2020. https://encyclopedia.ushmm.org/content/en/article/martin-niemoeller-first-they-came-for-the-socialists.

Platt, David. *A Compassionate Call to Counter-Culture*. Carol Stream, IL: Tyndale House Publishers, 2015.

Pornography + Sex Trafficking. https://stoptraffickingdemand.com/about/.

Rush, Benjamin. *Essays, Literary, Moral & Philosophical*. 2nd ed. Philadelphia, PA: Thomas & William Bradford, 1806.

———. *Letters of Benjamin Rush*. Vol. 1. Edited by L. H. Butterfield. Princeton, NJ: Princeton University Press, 1951.

Studd, C. T. "C. T. Studd > Quotes > Quotable Quote." Goodreads.com. Accessed April 14, 2020. http://www.goodreads.com/quotes/549103-only-one-life-twill-soon-be-past-only-what-s-done.

Billy Sunday as quoted in Wiersbe, Warren W. *Be Skillful: Tapping God's Guidebook to Fulfillment*. Wheaton, IL: Victor Books, 1996.

Tolkien, J. R. R. *The Lord of the Rings: The Fellowship of the Ring*. Rev. ed. New York, NY: Houghton Mifflin Company, 1966.

Voltaire as quoted in Cronk, Nicholas. *The Cambridge Companion to Voltaire*. Cambridge: Cambridge University Press, 2009.

Voltaire as quoted in Merritt, Daniel. "Voltaire's Prediction, Home, and the Bible Society: Truth or Myth? Further Evidence of Verification." CrossExamined.org. August 18, 2019. Accessed November 17, 2020. https://crossexamined.org/voltaires-prediction-home-and-the-bible-society-truth-or-myth-further-evidence-of-verification/#_ftnref3.

Wangerin, Jr., Walter. *Ragman and Other Cries of Faith*. San Francisco, CA: Harper & Row, 1984.

Nathaniel Ward as quoted in Marshall, Peter and David Manuel. *The Light and the Glory:1492-1793*. Grand Rapids, MI: Revell, 2009.

Webster, Noah. *History of the United States*. New Haven, CT: Durrie & Peck, 1832.

———. *The Holy Bible, Containing the Old and New Testaments, in the Common Version, With Amendments of the Language*. New Haven, CT: Durrie & Peck, 1833.

Wurmbrand, Richard. *Tortured for Christ*. Bartlesville, OK: Living Sacrifice Book Company, 1967.

Otto Zockler as quoted in Mead, Frank S., ed. *12,000 Religious Quotations*. 1965; Reprint, Grand Rapids, MI: Baker Book House, 1989.

ABOUT THE AUTHOR

Jonathan Macintyre has spent his adult life in ministry, primarily as a youth and young adults pastor, a worship leader, and leading missions all over the world. He attended Calvary Chapel Bible College and continued his education at Southern California Seminary, where he earned a Bachelor's in Biblical Studies and a Master's in Apologetics and Philosophy. He has a passion to teach God's Word, to disciple the youth, and to lead missions locally and abroad.

Made in the USA
Las Vegas, NV
14 August 2023

76088897R00125